CAREERS WITHOUT COLLEGE™

KIDS

by Maura Curless

Series developed by Peggy Schmidt

Peterson's

Princeton, New Jersey

A New Century Communications Book

Other titles in
this series include:

CARS

COMPUTERS

EMERGENCIES

FASHION

FITNESS

HEALTH CARE

MUSIC

Curless, Maura Rhodes, 1959–
    Kids / by Maura Curless.
        p.   cm.—(Careers without college)
    Summary: Provides information about five careers that involve contact with young people: caregiver, recreation instructor, salesperson, teacher aide, and museum or amusement park employee. Includes interviews with people in each field.
    ISBN 1-56079-251-5 (pbk.) : $7.95
    1. Child care—Vocational guidance—United States—Juvenile literature. [1. Vocational guidance.] I. Title. II. Series.
HQ778.7.U6C85   1993
649'.1'02373—dc20   93-7078
                                        CIP
                                         AC

Art direction: Linda Huber
Cover photo: Bryce Flynn Photography
Cover and interior design: Greg Wozney Design, Inc.
Composition: Bookworks Plus
Printed in the United States of America
10 9 8 7 6 5 4 3 2 1

Text Photo Credits
Color photo graphics: J. Gerard Smith Photography
Page xvi: © Design Concepts/Susan Lapides
Page 20: © Woodfin Camp & Associates, Inc./
    F. Fournier
Page 40: © Richard Hutchings
Page 58: © Woodfin Camp & Associates, Inc./Jacque
    Chenet
Page 78: © Woodfin Camp & Associates, Inc./Leif
    Skoogfors

ABOUT THIS SERIES

Careers Without College is designed to help those who don't have a four-year college degree (and don't plan on getting one any time soon) find a career that fits their interests, talents and personality. It's for you if you're about to choose your career—or if you're planning to change careers and don't want to invest a lot of time or money in more education or training, at least not right at the start.

Some of the jobs featured do require an associate degree; others only require on-the-job training that may take a year, some months or only a few weeks. In today's increasingly competitive job market, you may want to eventually consider getting a two- or maybe a four-year college degree in order to move up in a field.

Each title in the series features five jobs in a particular industry or career area. Some of them are "ordinary," others are glamorous. The competition to get into certain featured occupations is intense; as a balance, we have selected jobs under the same career umbrella that are easier to enter. Some of the other job opportunities within each field will be featured in future titles in this series.

Careers without College has up-to-date information that comes from extensive interviews with experts in each field. The format is designed for easy reading. Plus, each book gives you something unique: an insider look at the featured jobs through interviews with people who work in them now.

We invite your comments about the series, which will help us with future titles. Please send your correspondence to: Careers Without College, c/o Peterson's Guides, Inc., P.O. Box 2123, Princeton, NJ 08543-2123.

Peggy Schmidt has written about education and careers for twenty years. She is author of Peterson's best-selling *The 90-Minute Resume*.

ACKNOWLEDGMENTS

Special thanks to the professionals who dedicated their time, energy and expertise to providing information for this book.

Marianna Bagge, Director, National Academy of Nannies, Inc., Denver, Colorado

Ed Ball, Director, National Retail Hobby Stores Association, Chicago, Illinois

Bev Billingsley, Community Services Information Secretary, Delta College, Saginaw, Michigan

Carolyn Boos, Kings Island Amusement Park, Cincinnati, Ohio

Linda Cardinale, Assistant Communications Director, Toy Manufacturers of America, New York, New York

Linda Geigle, President, National Association of Family Day Care, Washington, D.C.

Capusine Jackson Grimes, Please Touch Museum, Philadelphia, Pennsylvania

Nancy Harvin, Support Staff Secretary, American Federation of Teachers, Washington, D.C.

Renee Henry, Director of Visitor Services, Please Touch Museum, Philadelphia, Pennsylvania

Nancy Holcomb, Owner, Toys and Co., Greensboro, North Carolina

Tom Iacobellis, Owner, Andy's Hobby Shop, Elmsford, New York

Max Lundberg, Director of Education for the Professional Ski Instructors Association, Lakewood, California

Bettina McGimsey, Project Manager, Center for Career Development in Early Care and Education, Wheelock College, Boston, Massachusetts

Randall McKeel, Executive Assistant, The Association for Youth Museums, Memphis, Tennessee

Patricia Olshefsky, Assistant Director, American Federation of Teachers, Washington, D.C.

Thom Peters, Vice President for Program Development, YMCA of Santa Clara Valley, San Jose, California

Steve Proffitt, Vice-president of Administration, the former King's Entertainment Company, Charlotte, North Carolina

Peggy Quinn, Accreditation Coordinator, National Association for the Education of Young Children, Washington, D.C.

George Zoombakis, Sales and Marketing Manager, Model Retailer Magazine, Chantilly, Virginia

WHAT'S IN THIS BOOK

WHY THESE "KIDS" CAREERS?

People who work with children recognize that not only are kids fun, they're tomorrow's movers and shakers. Kids must be protected and cared for, nurtured and taught skills that will help them become happy and productive adults. The days when parents could do all this on their own are long past. Now there are many adults who share in the up-bringing and education of young children. Most of them are driven by their enjoyment of being with young people to pursue kid-related careers, such as the five that are featured in this book:

- ❏ Caregiver
- ❏ Recreation instructor
- ❏ Toy or hobby store salesperson
- ❏ Preschool teacher or teacher aide
- ❏ Museum or amusement park staffer

Getting into these career areas does not require a four-year college degree. Employers are more interested in hiring people who have a natural talent for relating to children in ways they can understand and respect, who are enthusiastic and young at heart, who are able to keep their frustrations in check, and who really enjoy being around kids.

Hands-on experience—working as a camp counselor, as a YMCA volunteer, babysitter or youth group leader—is a definite plus for potential employees. Some coursework in early childhood education, child development and subjects such as first aid/CPR can be helpful in landing a job, as well as knowing how to do it well.

The five jobs discussed here involve working with kids in different capacities. Caregivers tend mostly to the little ones—infants to preschoolers. They may care for children in one family on a live-in or live-out basis, provide care for a small group of children in their own homes or work in a day care center. They do almost everything the parents would do to see that the children are fed, dressed, kept clean, entertained, stimulated and loved. Some caregivers prefer to work with older children in afterschool programs, such as those offered by YMCAs and some schools.

Recreation instructors usually have a special expertise that they enjoy teaching to children—from tots to teens. It may be swimming, gymnastics, skiing or any number of other athletic or even crafts activities. There are many job opportunities at recreation centers and other facilities that cater to kids, in vacation areas such as Club Meds and ski resorts, and in fitness centers designed especially for children.

Those who work in toy and hobby stores channel their interest in kids and kid things into selling. They make it their business to know what types of toys are appropriate for children of different ages and are so familiar with the products in their stores that they can help even the most confused customers choose the perfect gift for the kid in their life.

If working in a school environment is appealing, you will want to check out the possibility of being a teacher aide or a preschool teacher. Teacher aides are usually found in kindergartens and grade schools, though some junior high and high schools hire them as well. Many states require that preschool teachers do some college-level coursework, but it seldom takes more than a year to complete.

Finally, if you're more drawn to being involved in kids' activities, you may want to consider working in a children's museum or an amusement or theme park. In a museum you may greet visitors, supervise craft activities or demonstrate the exhibits and answer questions. In an amusement park, you may dress up as a cartoon character, operate rides, or, if you have musical talent, perform in shows.

Working with children can be exhilarating and exasperating, fulfilling and frustrating, physically demanding and emotionally draining. Depending on the area you choose, this field can send you in many directions. As a teacher aide, for instance, you may decide to get a degree and become a certified teacher; if you're a toy store employee, you may eventually set up your own store; if you're an employee of an amusement park or children's museum and prove yourself highly motivated and versatile, you may become involved in administration.

In addition to up-to-date information about each of these careers, you will get a highly personal hands-on sense of them by reading the interviews at the end of every chapter. Three people who are doing the job tell you what it's really like, and why they enjoy coming to work.

Before you begin learning about these careers, you may find a little inspiration by reading the stories of three people whose careers really took off. Then discover what the executive producer of the highly acclaimed television show, "Reading Rainbow," Dr. Twila Liggett, has to say about the challenge and satisfaction of working in a job that's kid connected.

When you finish reading this guide, you'll be well on your way to choosing the "kids" career that's right for you.

TWILA C. LIGGETT

on What It Takes to Work Successfully with Kids

There's hardly a kid who hasn't tuned in to the popular Public Broadcasting System television show "Reading Rainbow" to be led through the magical world of books by host Levar Burton. In what may seem an unlikely match, the so-called boob tube and the printed word come together brilliantly to encourage children to read. Since the

ix

show's debut in 1983, it has picked up three daytime Emmys: Best Series (1990), Best Videotape Editing (1991) and Best Directing (1992), as well as numerous awards for its creator, Twila C. Liggett, Ph.D.

The mastermind behind the critically acclaimed "Reading Rainbow" knew by the time she was in high school that she wanted to somehow educate kids. She had relatives who were teachers, and when she and her three younger sisters played school, she was the one who wielded the chalk and led the lessons. In fact, Dr. Liggett began her formal career as a music teacher in rural Nebraska, where she taught music in grades kindergarten through high school.

During this time, she fell in love with educating small children and went back to school to acquire her teaching degree for kindergarten and first and second grades. As time went on, her experience in the classroom drove home to her the importance of having qualified personnel in charge of schools, and she returned to college to obtain a degree in school administration. This spurred her on to acquire her doctorate, and while working toward her Ph.D. she held a few different jobs, including one writing grant proposals.

This job turned out to be a godsend for Liggett. Soon after she completed her Ph.D. she saw an ad for an opening at the Nebraska Public Television Network for someone who could write grant proposals. She was hired for the job, and the first thing she was asked was if she could write a proposal for a children's television show. Dr. Liggett responded that if she were going to select an area to focus on, she would choose getting kids to read. Using theories on how to motivate kids to read that she had developed while teaching, Dr. Liggett came up with the premise for "Reading Rainbow." Within two years, Dr. Liggett had acquired pilot funding for the show, for which she served as executive producer. By 1983, "Reading Rainbow" was on the air.

The unusual path Dr. Liggett's career took—from the classroom to the television studio—has given her a unique vantage point from which to view the world of children. She is testimony to the fact that often a toehold in a particular area can (with experience, further education and sheer determination) lead to career success. Here are her ideas about what it takes to be a good teacher, caregiver, leader and friend to children of all ages.

If you care about the future, working with children is probably one of the most important jobs you can have. It may sound almost trite, but it's so true: If you give children a good start in life—educationally as well as psychologically—you give them a foundation for learning for the rest of their lives. Conversely, if kids don't receive a good start, they don't have a chance. Having the opportunity to work with young children means being a contributor to our future.

I think that very soon there will be more and more places that provide child care, education and entertainment for children. And I believe it's good for kids to be in these settings, where they're involved and stimulated and doing things. The people working in these settings will need to have some experience with and commitment to kids and a willingness to get training. I feel this is going to come about because parents will simply demand it.

All of the jobs featured in this book in one way or another add to the stimulation and growth of kids—some more obviously than others. I once attended a seminar where a woman who owns an educational toy store spoke, and I was struck by her knowledge of children and her grasp of how they develop. Of course, the best start for this career lies in how the toy store owner chooses to stock the store— with children and learning in mind. Beyond that, I think being able to explain to parents how important educational toys are can be incredibly valuable. People who work in amusement parks and museums geared especially for young people also have an excellent opportunity to interact with children and stimulate their minds.

There are some caregivers who think that if they keep the children warm and dry and fed then they have met all of their needs. Of course, those things are important, but you've got to go beyond the basic creature comforts. It's not enough to plunk kids down in front of a television and set the stage for early couch potato-ism. A loving and educated caregiver, whether she's a nanny, an employee of a day care center or a family day care provider, stimulates kids with games, word play and puzzles. She reads storybooks and encourages her charges to participate in interactive social play with other children.

Verbal and mental stimulation are incredibly important in those early years. It's what enhances a child's intellectual curiosity and inquisitiveness, and without it, a child runs the risk of being delayed developmentally. In similar ways, preschool teachers also have a tremendous responsibility for young children who are developing social and mental skills. One main difference between them and caregivers is that the teacher may be working in a more structured setting.

I had several teacher aides when I was an educator, so I can speak from experience about that career. Having an aide in the classroom increases the adult-to-child ratio and gives students yet another adult to whom they can relate and take their problems. This is one of the greatest contributions the teacher aide brings to the development of children, particularly if she is working with a teacher who involves her and makes her part of the team. The well-used teacher aide can listen to kids read aloud, help them develop their writing skills and organize the classroom. Because the aide works closely with children, it helps if she understands what's going on with them at each age. Even though she's under the supervision of the teacher, she should go out on her own and get some books on child development and read them.

As for working with children as a recreation instructor, physical manipulation is very helpful for kids: It has been said that play is a child's work. Physical activity can help to enhance hand-eye coordination, which is especially important for little children when they begin to learn to read and write. And there are many social and emotional benefits to physical play. For instance, it helps to teach cooperation.

What does it take to work well with children? I think in many ways you need to have personality traits that are childlike qualities—inquisitiveness and a sense of wonder. People who spend time with children must enjoy life, and they must also enjoy kids and have an appreciation for the way they develop. There was a famous Swiss child psychologist, Jean Piaget, who once wrote that children are the true scientists because they wonder why and how come. It is wonderful for the grown-ups who interact with children to have that same quality—to wonder and ask why and to try new things.

Also important is the ability to help children learn to construct boundaries, and to creatively help them learn to choose in ways in which they feel safe as they venture into the real world. The people who are involved in the lives of children must also have a sense of openness and appreciation for children at every stage of their development, and they should not be negative about them. There are adults who talk down to children and see them as dumb—but kids aren't dumb. They may not figure out things the way an adult does, but, in fact, sometimes they are a little more creative than grown-ups.

People who work with children should also have an intellectual interest in the theories about child development. If you find yourself drawn to books and articles about children's levels of moral reasoning and growth stages, that would definitely be a clue to your own personal interest in being involved with kids in some way.

At the risk of sounding obvious, let me also add that you should genuinely like children. It's one thing to enjoy being around your little niece or the next-door neighbor's kid; it's another to actually work with groups of children on a day-to-day basis. One of the best ways to discover if you are truly meant to do this type of work is to get involved. For instance, there are places that provide afterschool child care that use volunteers from high schools. If you take advantage of such programs, you may actually be one up on the people who go through several years of college in, say, early childhood education and then come into the classroom as a student teacher, only to find out that they don't really enjoy being around children. By working part time or as a volunteer in a setting that includes lots of kids, you may find out much sooner than those student teachers whether or not you really are cut out for a career involving kids.

SUCCESS STORIES

Alexander Weber, Jr., Executive Vice President and General Manager, Kings Island theme park, Cincinnati, Ohio

Weber's first theme park job was operating a ride called The Monster at the Old Coney Island park in Cincinnati. He quickly moved on to become the full-time director of rides. Weber abandoned his architecture studies to dedicate himself to the theme park business. It paid off: He moved on to become park operations director for Carowinds, which straddles both North Carolina and South Carolina, general manager of Hanna Barbara Land near Houston, and then vice president and general manager of Great America in Santa Clara, California.

Barbara Meyerson, Director, Arizona Museum for Youth in Mesa, Arizona, and Vice President, Association of Youth Museums

At 12, Meyerson became the first junior aide at the Brooklyn Museum. She continued volunteering at the museum while studying art in college and even while teaching art at a nearby public school. When she and her husband moved to Arizona, Meyerson contacted a group she'd read about that was planning an art museum for children. The group liked her, handed her a bunch of brochures on other kids' museums in the country and let her loose. In the 12 years since, the museum has grown from a storefront facility to a city-owned museum with an operating budget of half a million dollars.

Shirley Bowman, Director, Parent-Child Center, Jacksonville, Florida

Bowman says, "Seeing children glow from accomplishment has always made my day." That's why she became a teacher aide at the Parent-Child Center, an organization devoted to helping parents interact with their children. She got an associate degree in early childhood education and obtained her CDA (Childhood Development Associate) credential. She later became a CDA representative. She went on to obtain her bachelor's and then her master's degree. Now she's second in command of the Parent-Child Center, which serves 120 families—the very place she began her career.

From changing diapers to zipping up snow-suits, singing lullabies to reading stories, gently scolding to giving hugs, a caregiver's duties are as diverse as the children she tends to. She wears many hats—playmate, teacher, disciplinarian, cook and chauffeur—but most important of all, she is a guardian and friend to the children she cares for.

The caregiver may be called a daycare provider or a staff member, a sitter, an au pair or a nanny. No matter what the title, the job itself is generally the same: looking after preschool youngsters—infants to five-year-olds (although some caregivers tend to the needs of school-age children when they're at home). She may work in a daycare center, where she is responsible for several youngsters at once; in her own home, a set-up known as family daycare; or in the

1

home of the children she cares for. Some caregivers actually live with the families they work for; room and board are part of their salary.

In any case, the children she oversees may spend a good part of their day with her. This allows a special closeness to develop between them—and it also means that the caregiver is a vital influence on the physical, emotional and intellectual development of her charges. For that reason, a caregiver must know about child development, nutrition, psychology and safety, among other things.

She must also know how to talk to and how to listen to parents so that both understand each other on important issues relating to the children, including eating and sleeping habits, temper tantrums and other behavior problems, and toilet training, to name a few. Practical knowledge is important to being a good caregiver, but just as critical is a sincere enjoyment of being in the company of babies or kids.

If you have always had an interest in talking to and playing with young children and find that they amuse you with their antics and view of the world, you have the right mindset for being a caregiver. Having great patience is also a big plus; few jobs are more likely to test the limits of your temper than caring for kids. They can be as demanding and ornery as they are giving and cheerful.

Whether you use your talents in a daycare center, in a child care business in your own home, or as a modernday Mary Poppins, you will play an important role in the lives of children through play and teaching. The hours can be long and the pay low, but if you prefer being with children than working with adults, you will no doubt find great satisfaction in your job.

What You Need to Know

- ❑ How infants, toddlers and preschoolers develop physically, emotionally and intellectually
- ❑ The fundamentals of childcare for different ages (how to change a diaper, warm a bottle, put a child down for a nap, etc.)
- ❑ Enough nutrition to be able to put together meals that not only will appeal to youngsters but are also appropriate for their age
- ❑ Songs, games, crafts and other activities that will amuse children
- ❑ The symptoms of illness in a child

Necessary Skills

- ❑ Child safety and first aid, CPR (a set of skills that can revive someone who has stopped breathing or whose heart has stopped)
- ❑ How to use equipment for children (strollers, car seats and so on)
- ❑ How to drive (if you have to take children to school, activities and on play dates)
- ❑ Good organizational skills, to structure a day's activities
- ❑ The ability to communicate effectively and diplomatically with parents regarding their youngster's behavior and progress
- ❑ Basic housekeeping and laundry skills (required by some families if you're a nanny)
- ❑ Gentle yet effective methods of discipline

Do You Have What It Takes?

- ❑ A genuine love of children and concern for their well-being
- ❑ A willingness to be open with affection
- ❑ A calm, reassuring manner
- ❑ Patience and compassion for the frustrations a child endures while growing and learning

- ❏ A sense of fairness (particularly when dealing with children in groups)
- ❏ An ability to talk to children in language they understand and with a tone of voice they are receptive to
- ❏ A knack for entertaining, amusing and otherwise engaging a child's attention
- ❏ An even temperament
- ❏ Great patience
- ❏ Good judgment about what's safe and what's not
- ❏ Common sense about how much monitoring and hands-on help a child needs

Physical Attributes

- ❏ Stamina (the hours can be long and children energetic)
- ❏ Good physical condition (you will be bending, picking up, walking and running)
- ❏ Good health (parents will depend on you to be available so they can go to work)
- ❏ Good personal hygiene (not only for the health of the children, but to set a good example for them)

Education

A high school diploma or graduate equivalency diploma (GED) is often required in daycare centers. Coursework in child development or early childhood education is a plus in getting hired. A number of private schools and community colleges offer nanny training programs and often placement services for those who successfully complete them.

Licenses Required

Some states require workers in commercial daycare centers to have a Child Development Associate (CDA) credential, which is awarded by the Council for Early Childhood Professional Recognition (on successful completion of a year-long program of classroom study and field-

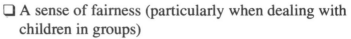

work). Providers of family day care usually must meet their state's licensing requirements; information on these is available from the state office of childcare or division of social services. Caregivers who are employed by families are not required to have any license.

Competition for jobs: average
Caregiver jobs are expected to remain plentiful for some time as parents—particularly moms—work full-time and thus need day-long, quality care for their kids. For this reason, a professional in the field of childcare who has made an effort to gain some experience and training should have no trouble securing a choice job. What's more, there is a high level of turnover because families relocate and their needs change, and women who enter the field when they're young may leave when they marry and start families of their own.

◆ **Job Outlook**

Entry-level job: daycare staff member, family daycare provider or nanny (also called sitter, caregiver and au pair)
Your job title will depend on whether you are an employee of a center or of a private family, or if you are an independent business owner. In any case, your job responsibilities will be essentially the same; what changes are the number of children you are responsible for at any one time.

◆ **The Ground Floor**

All caregivers

❏ Prepare and serve nutritious meals and snacks
❏ Change diapers, wash dirty hands, wipe runny noses and perform other hygiene-related tasks
❏ Put children down for naps
❏ Plan and carry out inside and outside play activities, including reading books, doing crafts, playing games, visiting playgrounds
❏ Demonstrate and teach good manners and hygiene
❏ Keep parents informed about child's behavior, progress and problems

◆ **On-the-Job Responsibilities**

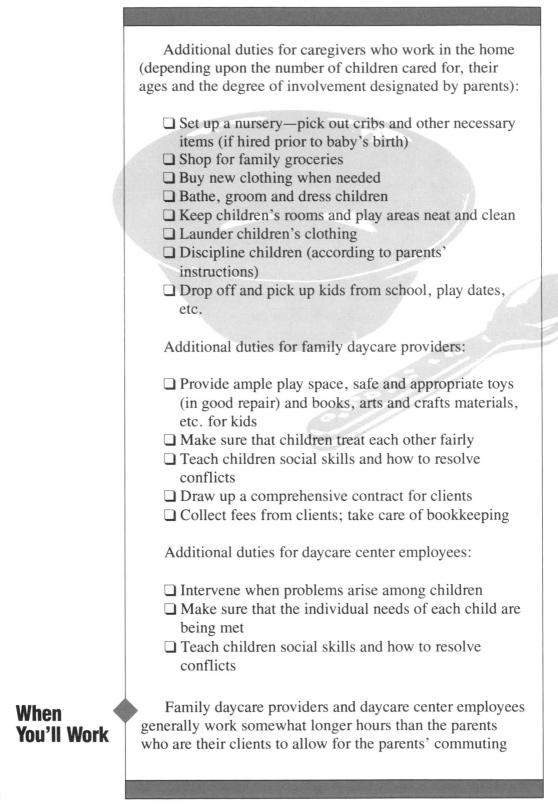

Additional duties for caregivers who work in the home (depending upon the number of children cared for, their ages and the degree of involvement designated by parents):

❑ Set up a nursery—pick out cribs and other necessary items (if hired prior to baby's birth)
❑ Shop for family groceries
❑ Buy new clothing when needed
❑ Bathe, groom and dress children
❑ Keep children's rooms and play areas neat and clean
❑ Launder children's clothing
❑ Discipline children (according to parents' instructions)
❑ Drop off and pick up kids from school, play dates, etc.

Additional duties for family daycare providers:

❑ Provide ample play space, safe and appropriate toys (in good repair) and books, arts and crafts materials, etc. for kids
❑ Make sure that children treat each other fairly
❑ Teach children social skills and how to resolve conflicts
❑ Draw up a comprehensive contract for clients
❑ Collect fees from clients; take care of bookkeeping

Additional duties for daycare center employees:

❑ Intervene when problems arise among children
❑ Make sure that the individual needs of each child are being met
❑ Teach children social skills and how to resolve conflicts

When You'll Work

Family daycare providers and daycare center employees generally work somewhat longer hours than the parents who are their clients to allow for the parents' commuting time to and from their jobs. Some family daycare providers may offer help to parents who work late night, early morning or weekend shifts, or provide only part-time care for a few hours in the morning or the afternoon. Nannies generally have the longest hours of all: They often begin their day early—in time to prepare breakfast for the children—and do not finish work until the last child has been put to bed.

◆ **Time Off**

Generally, daycare centers and family daycare providers operate on the same schedules as most businesses; most are closed on weekends and major holidays. Nannies, however, may be expected to work weekends or parts of weekends (depending on the parents' work schedules) and travel with families on business or pleasure to help care for the children.

Vacation days vary for employees of daycare centers; a typical setup would be one week off the first year, two weeks off for the second year and three weeks off per each year after that. As independent business people, family daycare providers can establish whatever vacation policies they feel are reasonable and fair.

Nannies who are placed through agencies or organizations that have contracts with their client families are usually entitled to one or two weeks' paid vacation a year, as well as paid holidays. Those who are hired independently by parents are well advised to have employers put the number and timing of paid days in writing before they accept a job offer.

◆ **Perks**

❏ Dress is casual and comfortable (occasionally nannies wear uniforms)
❏ Luxury of setting your own hours (for family daycare providers)
❏ Use of a car (for many live-in nannies)
❏ Travel (for many nannies who are asked to accompany their families on vacations and other trips)

Who's Hiring

❑ Daycare centers, including national chains and small mom-and-pop businesses
❑ Church-run daycare centers
❑ YMCAs (the largest employer of child care professionals in the U.S.)
❑ Individual families (who may be clients of family daycare providers or employers of nannies)

Places You'll Go

There is no job-related travel opportunities for family daycare providers and daycare center employees.

Nannies who work for well-to-do families may be required or asked to accompany them to vacation spots, family gatherings or on business trips.

Surroundings

Most daycare centers feature large, cheerful rooms decorated in bright colors and furnished with shelves for toys; educational materials; books and arts and crafts supplies; tot-sized desks, chairs and tables; cribs and so forth. Most have outdoor playgrounds with swings, sandboxes, jungle gyms and the like. Some nonprofit daycare centers that are located in inner-city neighborhoods may have less space and older equipment and toys.

The work environment of the family daycare provider is basically what she makes of it. Some providers allow "their" children the run of the house; others keep the kids confined to several rooms, such as the playroom, the bedrooms of their own youngsters, the kitchen and the family room. In any event, the rooms must be set up according to safety standards (dangerous objects kept out of reach, electrical outlets protected by safety plugs, stairways blocked off with gates, etc.) and furnished with toys, books and so forth. Most providers set up their backyards for children to play in and erect fences, swings, sandboxes and play areas.

The work environment of nannies varies widely. Some are employed in spacious homes where they have their own room, bathroom or even apartment. Others may work in a more confined space such as an apartment and even share a room or bathroom with the kids.

The weekly salary of a daycare center employee ranges from about $160 to more than $330. Family daycare providers typically charge by the week. This figure varies widely according to region and number of hours care is provided. The ages of the children figures in as well: Providers often charge more for caring for an infant than for a toddler or preschooler. Live-in nannies may make anywhere from $100 to $400 per week, plus room and board.

Generally speaking, parents who work in major metropolitan areas, particularly on the East and West coasts, are willing to pay the most for good childcare.

Dollars and Cents

There is no formal career ladder for family daycare providers or nannies. If your family daycare service is in high demand (that is, you have more "customers" than spaces available) or your nanny experience is extensive, you may be able to charge higher rates or command a higher salary. Successful family daycare providers may at some point hire help and become a manager as well as a provider. Employees of large daycare centers may get promoted to supervisory or administrative positions; such advancement usually requires a two- or a four-year degree in child development, teaching or some other related area.

Moving Up

Employment opportunities abound from coast to coast, although live-in nannies are most likely to find work in major metropolitan areas, where both parents work and command good salaries.

Where the Jobs Are

Many community colleges and high schools with night classes for adults offer courses in child development, nutrition and related topics. You can get a list of schools accredited by the American Council of Nanny Schools by contacting the organization at Delta College, Attention: Joy Shelton, Room A-74, University Center, Michigan, 48710, 517-686-9417. (Delta College also offers a one-year certification program for nannies, a two-year associate degree

Schooling

program and a science degree program as well as a placement service for graduates.)

The Male/Female Equation

Most caregivers are women, particularly those who oversee very young children. The main deterrent for men in the field is the low pay—particularly for those who have or who intend to have a family of their own to provide for.

Making Your Decision: What to Consider

The Bad News

❏ Hours can be long, and the work physically and emotionally demanding
❏ Pay is low
❏ There is virtually no opportunity for advancement

The Good News

❏ Children are often more pleasant to be around than adults—as hard as it can be, the work is usually fun
❏ Live-in nannies have the advantage of free room and board
❏ Child care lacks the cutthroat competitiveness of many other professions

More Information Please

National Association for Family Day Care (NAFDC)
1331-A Pennsylvania Avenue NW
Suite 348
Washington, D.C. 20004
800-359-3817

A networking organization for state and local family day-care associations. NAFDC also offers memberships to individuals for an annual fee of $20. Members receive a bimonthly newsletter and have access to a wealth of information regarding how to set up a family daycare practice.

Child Care Employee Project
6536 Telegraph Avenue
Suite A-201
Oakland, California 94609-1114
415-653-9889

A nonprofit advocacy group for the child care workforce—particularly regarding wages. Members receive a newsletter, updates on childcare policies and discounts on printed material put out by the organization. Regular memberships are $15 per year for child care workers.

National Academy of Nannies, Inc.
1681 South Dayton Street
Denver, Colorado 80231
303-333-NANI or 800-222-NANI

The first private nanny training school in the United States and one of the best. NANI offers a year's worth of comprehensive training in all aspects of childcare as well as opportunities for practical experience. Upon completion of the program, students take exams and then are aided in their job search by the school.

International Nanny Association (INA)
P.O. Box 26522
Austin, Texas 78755
512-454-6462

A private, nonprofit educational organization for nannies INA offers health and liability insurance options to members as well as a bimonthly newsletter. The association also sponsors a yearly conference. Basic membership is $35 per year.

The Council for Early Childhood Professional Recognition
1341 G Street, NW
Washington, D.C. 20005-3105
202-265-9090 or 800-424-4310

Through the CECPR, caregivers may obtain the Child Development Associate (CDA) credential, which is recognized by 49 states as a qualification for employment in a childcare center. The Council also publishes a free newsletter three times a year and puts out educational material for CDA candidates.

WHAT IT'S REALLY LIKE

Stacy Pillow, 20,
live-in nanny,
Dayton, Ohio
Years in the field: two

How did you get started as a nanny?
After a semester of college, I realized I wasn't ready for it.
And I was paying for it on my own. I decided I wanted to
be a nanny. I heard about the National Academy of Nannies, Inc., in Denver—a school for nannies—and applied.
It took me about four months to complete the application. I
had to include my driving record; a criminal record, if I
had any; five recommendation letters; five references who
were sent a questionnaire about me; and my high school
transcripts.

What's involved in NANI training?
For a year I lived with a sponsorship family that had two
children. I cared for the kids all day and went to school
four nights a week from 6:30 to 9:30 P.M. I took classes in
child development, family relations, nutrition, pre-
academics (which is learning about the math and reading
levels of children of different ages so that you can help

kids with their homework); there was also a class in working with children who have special needs.

The family relations course covered the employee/employer relationship, which can be a pretty sensitive one in this field, especially for nannies who live with the families that employ them.

How did you find your first family?
Usually NANI can help place you, but as luck would have it, there were no jobs available through NANI when I finished. So I decided to look on my own and landed a job in Vail, Colorado. I was working six days a week, with few benefits and little time off. When I did get a break, I visited my parents and through talking with them realized it was time to move on; after my vacation I gave notice.

So how did you get your second job?
I went back to NANI, and this time they had tons of families in need of nannies. I interviewed and was offered several jobs. The one I took was with my current family. I flew out and stayed for a week to get to know them. It's a single mom with three children ages two, four and nine.

What is special about this job?
In the last family I was little more than hired help; here I feel very welcome. I feel like I'm part of the team since it's a single-parent family. And my boss is most appreciative of everything I do.

What are your living conditions like?
I have my own room, and I share a bathroom with the three children. I have a phone in my room. I have access to the kitchen. I have paid medical insurance, paid sick days and taxes taken out of my pay, plus use of a car.

What do you like most about your job?
I love the children. My favorite thing about this job is teaching the kids and learning from them. They're like little sponges. Everyone helps clean; even the little boys put away their laundry.

Is there anything you don't like?
Sometimes it's hard to have a live-in job because although you have your privacy, the work is just behind your bedroom door. On your days off, you can just lay around in

your room, but you feel like a bum because you hear everyone else up. I don't have a curfew, but it's hard walking in
really late at night. Still, I would say a live-in job would be
the best way to start out. You learn so much living with the
family.

What is a typical day like for you?
I start work between 7:45 and 8:00 A.M. I give the kids
breakfast and send the older one to school. I take the four-
year-old to preschool. Then I straighten up and clean. Later
I pick up the four-year-old; we come home and I fix lunch.
Afterward we may play a game. Then I put both children
down for a nap. The four-year-old gets up first, and we
work on numbers or read until the baby's up. When the
nine-year-old gets home from school, we all have a snack,
then I help her with her homework. When that's done, we
often do an arts and crafts project, or, if it's been a rough
day, we pop in a video and veg out. I often get dinner
started. The mom gets home around 7 P.M. As soon as she's
in the house, I'm off work, although we usually all eat
together. Then I might go running or swimming or bike
riding.

**What advice would you give to someone still in high
school who is contemplating becoming a nanny?**
I would highly suggest nanny school. You don't need it to
get a job, but I think it's for your own good: I learned so
much at school. It's made a difference in my job—I'm con-
fident and feel good about what I do.

Annette Hansen, 31,
family daycare provider,
Dale City, Virginia
Years in field: six

How did you get started?
I was living in Washington state, and my own child care
provider was moving. One of the other parents in her group,
who also happened to be the child care licenser for the area,
asked me if I knew anyone who could take over. I was
working at the time, but my salary was low. With the cost

of child care for my own kids, I wasn't making all that much. I figured out the finances and decided to give it a whirl. I found it was something I really enjoyed.

What did you have to do to establish your business?
In Washington, you're required by law to have a license to provide child care. I applied for that and also went through a criminal history check, as did my husband. My home had to meet specific safety standards, and I was required to have certain things, like a minimum amount of space for a play area. Because I had two kids of my own, I already had much of what I needed.

Clients were no problem because several of the people in the daycare home that was closing up were actively seeking a provider. We had formal interviews and I threw together a contract and a philosophy sheet, with general information about my hours and fees. A lot of my ideas came from handbooks and literature provided by the state. I was allowed six kids including my own, and I started right out with a full house of four full-timers, plus some part-timers who were there for less than three hours each.

Did you encounter any problems?
When I started out, I was naive in some ways. For example, in my contract I wrote out a schedule of what I was going to do with the kids hour by hour. I have to laugh looking back because lots of unexpected things pop up during the day—hurt fingers, dirty diapers, arguments among the kids. I learned right away that you have to be open to letting the day go and flow.

What prepared you for being a family daycare provider?
I'm the oldest of five girls. When my parents divorced, my next youngest sister and I had a lot of responsibility in caring for the others, who were much younger. I also began babysitting at the age of 12. I had my first child at 21, so the remainder of my experience has come from parenting my own kids.

About six months after I went into business I attended a class for daycare providers at the local community college. It was a real eye-opener for me; I learned aspects of child development I wasn't aware of, how to handle the account-

15

ing and how to look at the job as a profession. I also acquired a support network of other providers. We shared different experiences we'd had with all sorts of things—temper tantrums, problems with parents, the bookkeeping. And I learned about accreditation and associations for providers. That helped me a lot when I moved to Virginia and had to start over after about 17 months of being in business.

How did setting up your business in Virginia differ from the first time around?
Getting started was much the same as in Washington—getting zoning permits and a license, which involved a criminal record check and a three-hour interview with the state licensing authority, among other things. The hard part was getting clients. I put up index cards at local grocery stores and also put an ad in the paper. But it took four months to fill up all my spaces.

What's a typical day like?
Kids arrive between 6:15 and 7 A.M. We have breakfast around 7:50. While my own children get ready for school, we have free play. Once I get my kids off to the bus, it's time for the others to brush their teeth. One day a week I make sure we stay home and enjoy the playroom. Other days, we have planned activities outside the house. When my daughter gets home from kindergarten we have lunch, then the little kids go down for a nap. Around 4:15 P.M. everyone starts waking up and we have an afternoon snack. By then the parents start coming to pick up their kids.

What do you like most about what you're doing?
That I feel needed. My "parents" are real happy with me and respect what I'm doing. And the children need me. They need to feel good about who they are to help build their self-esteem. Since their moms and dads can't be there for them all the time, I'm the one who is there for them. It's great, but sometimes it has its drawbacks because you can't give your own kids all the one-on-one you'd like to. The benefits are that they learn to share, to live in a family situation where everyone has to take turns, to talk out problems with others.

What advice can you offer to someone who wants to become a family daycare provider?
First look within yourself: You have to know who you are, be easygoing, that is, able to go with the flow and be incredibly patient. The next step is education, but I don't believe you have to have a four-year degree. Use your community resources to find relevant courses in childcare, nutrition and so forth. Accreditation is another step up. This helps you make sure your home meets national standards. It's a matter of pride, shows you're committed and is comforting to prospective parent-clients. I would also suggest seeking out a local association for family day care providers such as our Prince William Family Childcare Association, which I'm president of. These groups can help new providers set up their business and serve as a support network.

Michael R. Loya, 26,
youth and family associate program director,
Southwest YMCA of Santa Clara Valley,
Saratoga, California
Years in the field: 12

How did you get involved with taking care of children?
When I was a freshman in high school I worked as a teacher aide in a YMCA afterschool childcare program. By the time I graduated, I wanted the Y to be my career, but I wanted to do more than be a teacher aide. So I attended community college to get the coursework required to become a qualified teacher, and then a director.

After completing it, I was put in charge of a YMCA-based school-age child care center at an elementary school. During this time I decided I wanted to progress even more, so I attended college for a year and took general courses. For financial reasons I quit after a year. Soon afterward I was given the director title of the San Miguel Center, a YMCA-based childcare center for children ages 5 to 12. It's fully licensed by the state of California.

17

As a director, how much did you interact with the kids?
A lot. I only did about one hour of administration a day. I spent the other seven plus hours working with kids. I planned and carried out a range of activities for them—crafts, music, cooking. After a year, I moved into my current position.

This YMCA has six childcare centers, and I substituted at all of them before choosing the one I wanted to head. When I subbed at the Fammatre Center, which is for kids ages 5 to 12, I hated it. It was very poorly run and there was a tremendous amount of staff turnover. But I decided to take it because I wanted to turn things around. I've been here for four years; two years ago I was promoted to associate youth and family program director. I now supervise two childcare centers as well two teen leadership clubs.

Why are you interested in working with kids?
I'm a big kid myself. I tell people that I enjoy my work because I can wear jeans and throw a football around all day. Interacting with kids is the real plus. In the future, I see myself working mostly with teens. They're fascinating people; they have a lot to offer, and there's no one to listen to them. They arc also at a time in their lives when they're having a lot of problems, and I like to give them support. It's like having a lot of little brothers and sisters. My goal is to supervise and become executive director of a youth camp.

Is there anything you find difficult about this career?
The hours are long: My average day lasts from 7 A.M. to 8 P.M.. And I'm definitely not in this for the money. The average pay here for a teacher is $7 to $8 an hour. For a director it can average about $10 an hour. I'm exceeding that, but it's still hard. I also have to deal with a lack of respect sometimes. I think society sees us as babysitters.

Describe the program you run.
We're an education service that is basically a supplement to the schools. We have a hands-on science program and youth sports and fitness programs.

Is it typical for YMCA employees to continue on with the organization?
I'd say about 25 to 35 percent of them stay with it and pursue it as a career, as I have. The nice thing about the Y is that it's very good about taking care of its own.

Is it hard being a man in child care?
We have to prove ourselves more than the women do. It took a year or two for the parents to feel comfortable with me. And I'm careful to never leave myself alone in a room with children without another adult there. We need more men in childcare. A lot of the kids I work with are from single-parent families; they rarely see their dads, so I'm the stable male in their lives. One plus to being a man is that kids will listen to a deep voice. I think by working with kids I'm training to be a good father. If I can calm down 32 screaming kids, I'll be able to handle my own children some day.

What does it take to succeed in this profession?
It takes a special person to work with kids. You need to bring something new in each day—a book, a game—because kids need to have as much stimulation as possible. And, of course, you need to bring a sense of fun with you.

Recreation instructors make a career out of child's play. Whether they're bouncing balls and watching their charges reach out for them, demonstrating the correct way to do a handstand or guiding small feet along a balance beam, they spend their time engaged in physical activities that are fun and involving. What's more, they take satisfaction in knowing they're helping to build and improve upon the skills of tomorrow's athletes.

Recreation instructors work with youngsters of all ages in a wide variety of ways. Some are employed by special play programs designed for infants and toddlers (and usually their parents). Others may teach children specific activities such as skiing, gymnastics or martial arts, or they may coach softball or soccer. Public parks and recreation centers, YMCAs, private clubs and vacation spots that cater to families are all potential places of employment for recreation instructors.

This career is not all play and no work, however. Besides teaching, recreation instructors set up class schedules and plan out each session. They make sure that the area in which they are teaching is safe for kids and for the activity. Before class they set up necessary equipment or materials. Afterward, even though they may get kids involved in restoring things to order, instructors ultimately are responsible for cleanups.

Those who move up to become supervisors, or who own and operate their own facility, for instance, buy into a franchise such as Gymboree, have to take care of business—hiring, budgets, bill-paying, advertising and all the other baggage that comes with owning a company.

Above all, recreation instructors manage to keep an eye on sometimes large groups of busy, pint-sized bodies, on the lookout for those having trouble with the activity—and for those making trouble for other kids. For this reason, recreation instructors often are hired more for their love of children and their ability to deal with them successfully than for their skills or training in a specific sport or activity—although practical experience is definitely a plus. More important are a knack for communicating with kids, an understanding of the physical and emotional differences among age groups and a sparkling, upbeat personality. It also helps to have spent a lot of time with kids babysitting, volunteering for youth groups or counseling at summer camps.

If you truly like children and get a kick out of seeing a little face light up when its owner succeeds, be it a toddler who finally catches a ball or a pre-teen who performs her first perfect somersault; if you have a flair for explaining and demonstrating things to children of different ages; if you are patient and reliable and able to walk the fine line between being the adult in charge and your charges' best pal, you have all the makings of a first-rate recreation instructor.

What You Need to Know

- ❏ The differences among children of specific ages in terms of physical capabilities, coordination, attention span, emotional maturity, ability to process new information and follow instructions
- ❏ How to motivate children and keep them involved and interested in an activity
- ❏ How to discipline children effectively (without using threats or extreme punishment)

Necessary Skills

- ❏ Good communication skills (the ability to talk with kids without talking down to them, to establish that you're the boss as well as a buddy, and, the ability to listen)
- ❏ Effective teaching tactics—both with words and through demonstration
- ❏ Knowing when to switch gears during a teaching session (for instance, if an activity is proving too frustrating or doesn't seem to appeal to the kids)
- ❏ How to control and watch over a number of kids at once
- ❏ The basics of safety and first aid
- ❏ Some experience playing the sport or activity yourself (usually)
- ❏ How to structure classes for various age groups
- ❏ For business owners: budgeting, hiring, advertising and other essentials for keeping a company going

Do You Have What It Takes?

- ❏ Upbeat, outgoing, energetic personality
- ❏ Spontaneity (the ability to recognize when a spur-of-the-moment change of lesson plan is needed to keep youngsters interested)
- ❏ Creativity (you should be inventive at coming up with games and exercises kids find fun)

❏ Patience
❏ A love of play
❏ A flair for teaching

Physical Attributes

❏ Nonsmoker
❏ Good personal hygiene (you'll be a role model for your students)
❏ Good physical condition and plenty of stamina (if you're teaching a sport or similar activity)

Education

A high school diploma is almost always necessary—particularly for positions that involve on-site training programs.

Licenses Required

Some recreation instructors are expected to be certified in CPR (a set of skills that can revive a person who has stopped breathing or whose heart has stopped). It may help, although it is rarely required, to be certified to teach a specific sport if such a credential is available (for instance, swimming instructors may receive training through the American Red Cross; gymnastics instructors can be certified by the United States Gymnastics Federation). Often, training and certification are provided by the employer.

Job Outlook

Competition for jobs: somewhat competitive

With more moms working, afterschool programs have proliferated, opening up jobs for recreation instructors of all types. There is also an increasing interest by children to hone the skills they may be taught only briefly in school by taking activity-specific classes. Vacation spots such as ski areas or spas have recognized a trend toward families who travel together, and they are developing special programs just for kids. Parents are also becoming vigilant about the physical development and socialization of their kids, and so are filling up the enrollment lists of infant and toddler play programs such as Discovery Zone and Kidsports, nationwide activity centers that focus on fitness for kids.

Entry-level job: recreation instructor

Some instructors begin as volunteers or part-timers, moving onto the payroll as they acquire the experience and skills to run their own classes—either by going through a training program at the facility where they are teaching or by aiding and observing other instructors. From there they may move up to supervise other instructors or choose to own and operate their own facility (if they work for a franchise, for instance).

◆ **The Ground Floor**

Beginners

◆ **On-the-Job Responsibilities**

❑ Check all materials and equipment to determine if they are in good repair and that there is enough to go around prior to class
❑ Make sure all kids in class are registered to be there
❑ Collect fees (sometimes)
❑ Conduct the teaching session, usually according to a pre-planned schedule
❑ See that all children are picked up by parents or a person approved by the parents
❑ Straighten up facility
❑ Field parents' questions regarding children's behavior, problems and progress

Supervisors and Facility Owners

❑ Hire, train and fire instructors
❑ Work out class and instructor schedules
❑ Develop new programs
❑ Handle administrative duties such as accounting and budget planning, promotion and advertising and managing facility maintenance

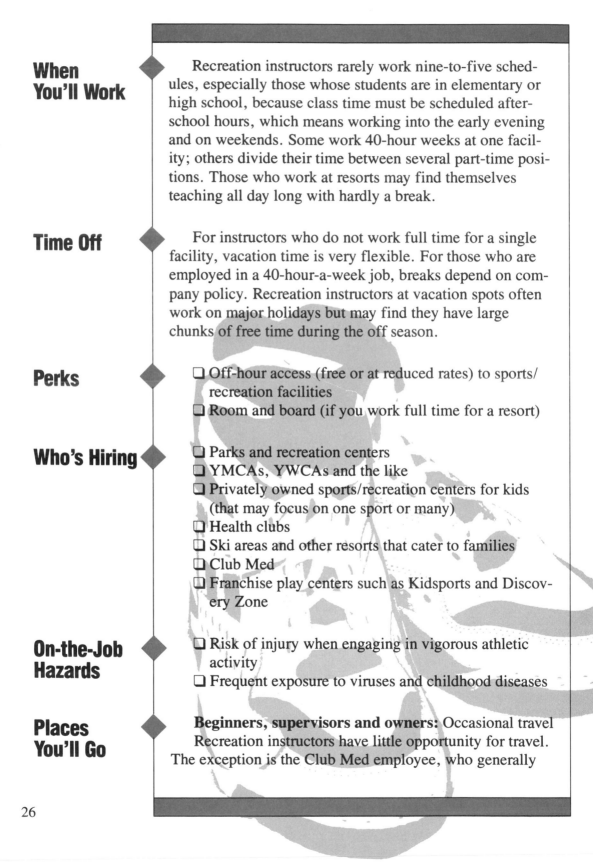

When You'll Work

Recreation instructors rarely work nine-to-five schedules, especially those whose students are in elementary or high school, because class time must be scheduled after-school hours, which means working into the early evening and on weekends. Some work 40-hour weeks at one facility; others divide their time between several part-time positions. Those who work at resorts may find themselves teaching all day long with hardly a break.

Time Off

For instructors who do not work full time for a single facility, vacation time is very flexible. For those who are employed in a 40-hour-a-week job, breaks depend on company policy. Recreation instructors at vacation spots often work on major holidays but may find they have large chunks of free time during the off season.

Perks

❑ Off-hour access (free or at reduced rates) to sports/ recreation facilities
❑ Room and board (if you work full time for a resort)

Who's Hiring

❑ Parks and recreation centers
❑ YMCAs, YWCAs and the like
❑ Privately owned sports/recreation centers for kids (that may focus on one sport or many)
❑ Health clubs
❑ Ski areas and other resorts that cater to families
❑ Club Med
❑ Franchise play centers such as Kidsports and Discovery Zone

On-the-Job Hazards

❑ Risk of injury when engaging in vigorous athletic activity
❑ Frequent exposure to viruses and childhood diseases

Places You'll Go

Beginners, supervisors and owners: Occasional travel
Recreation instructors have little opportunity for travel. The exception is the Club Med employee, who generally

switches "camps" every six months and may go from Florida to the Bahamas in a single year.

The work environment of the recreation instructor can range from a noisy, bustling ball field to a quiet, snow-covered mountain to a music-saturated indoor play space decorated in bright colors and filled with kid-sized seating and equipment.

◆ **Surroundings**

Recreation instructors may be paid by the hour, by the class or according to a yearly salary. Employees of YMCAs, park and recreation centers and similar facilities may make as little as $7 or $8 an hour or as much as $12 to $14 per hour—even those in managerial positions. Instructors of specific sports may increase their earnings by teaching private lessons: It isn't uncommon for swimming teachers to charge $100 for five half-hour lessons or for ski instructors to draw from $15 to $30 for an hour-long, one-on-one lesson on the slopes. Club Med employees who work in the Petit Club (for two- and three-year-olds), the Mini Club (for kids ages four to seven), the Kids Club (for eight- to ten-year-olds) or the Teen Club start at $450 a week. They also get room and board. Ski areas and resorts often have similar arrangements.

◆ **Dollars and Cents**

Entrepreneurs who wish to own their own business will have to have enough money on hand to get the company rolling—for rent, employee salaries, necessary licensing, equipment, advertising and promotion. Buying into an existing company is often a good way to do this: Start-up costs for franchises range from as little as $30,000 to a six-figure investment.

The corporate ladder of the kids' recreation industry is more like a stepstool. In some cases, instructors may have the opportunity to move up to a management position—overseeing a group of kids' instructors in a larger facility,

◆ **Moving Up**

for instance—but beyond that there is little opportunity for growth. On the plus side, recreation instructors can make extra money by freelancing as private instructors or, with enough experience and capital, start their own business or buy into a franchise.

Where the Jobs Are

Where there are kids, there are jobs for people who instruct them. From coast to coast, 968 YMCAs and 5,000 local parks and recreation centers hire people to work with kids. Teachers of seasonal sports may be somewhat limited. Jobs for ski instructors clearly are limited to the Rocky Mountain states, New England and other parts of the country that have ski-worthy weather and terrain. Tennis and golf teachers are more likely to find steady work in the warmer climates of the West Coast and Florida (although indoor sports facilities make year-round employment possible in other parts of the country). Club Med employees must interview in New York, but after that they are sent all over the world.

Training

More often than not, recreation instructors receive their most valuable training after being hired. YMCAs, for instance, have their own training programs for new employees. Many individual sports, such as swimming, gymnastics and tennis, have certification programs, however, that focus on the nuts and bolts of teaching children effectively and safely; information on these courses may be obtained by contacting the individual sports associations.

The Male/Female Equation

In jobs that focus on very young children—infants, toddlers and preschoolers—women dominate, although employers often are eager to hire men for these spots to give kids a more well-rounded experience. The numbers of men and women working with older children are not significantly different.

The Bad News

❑ Salaries are often low
❑ Long hours
❑ Little room for advancement
❑ Working with kids can be physically wearing and frustrating

The Good News

❑ Potential to make extra bucks by teaching privately
❑ Flexibility of work schedules and vacation time
❑ With experience and savings, entrepreneurs may start their own business
❑ The opportunity to make a career out of a favorite hobby, sport or skill

◆ **Making Your Decision: What to Consider**

Club Med Human Resources
212-755-6458

By calling this number, you can find out everything you need to know about how to apply for work at a Club Med village, including the personal information you need to provide, where to send it and how to arrange for an interview.

YMCA of the USA
National Vacancy List
101 North Wacker Drive
Chicago, Illinois 60606
800-872-9622

A list of job openings in YMCAs nationwide, published bimonthly and available for a yearly subscription fee of $20. The list includes a complete job description of each opening, its location, starting salary and contact person.

◆ **More Information Please**

The following associations offer sport-specific certification programs, including workshops, training and exams throughout the country.

United States Professional Tennis Association
One USPTA Center
3535 Briarpark Drive
Houston, Texas 77042
713-978-7782

United States Professional Tennis Registry
P.O. Box 4739
Hilton Head Island, South Carolina 29938
800-421-6289

United States Gymnastics Federation
Pan American Plaza, Suite 300
201 S. Capitol Avenue
Indianapolis, Indiana 46225
317-237-5050

SwimAmerica
American Swimming Coaches Association
304 S.E. 20th Street
Fort Lauderdale, Florida 33316
800-356-2722

Professional Ski Instructors Association
133 South Van Gordon Drive
Lakewood, Colorado 80228
303-987-9390

Karen King, 37,
swim school director,
Mission Bay Sports Complex,
Boca Raton, Florida;
and national director, SwimAmerica Training
Years in the field: five

How did you get started?

I was living in Virginia when my youngest son was ready to learn to swim; he was four. Unfortunately, there was no teacher—the instructor had left the class in the lurch—so I offered to teach lessons. I started working as a basic swim instructor. Then more and more people wanted to take lessons, so I became interested in making this a career. During the first three months of teaching I took the SwimAmerica training program—a goal-oriented method of teaching that helps children learn to swim quickly. I went to Fort Lauderdale for a week to do the training; in fact, I was one of the first people to take the course. When I went back to Virginia I established a summer swim school. I started out with 75 kids; by the end of the third year I had over 700.

What responsibilities did that first job entail?

I took registrations and placed children in the appropriate

classes. I also hired instructors and trained them. I had two moms who worked with the youngest kids, teaching them to put their face in the water and other basics. The rest of the teachers were senior swim team members—top-ranked swimmers in the state. I handled advertising, too.

Before you took the SwimAmerica training had you had any other preparation for this job?
Yes. I grew up near water, on Long Island in New York and swam at the public beaches. Also, I was in college for a few years in rural Illinois. I was there on scholarship, majoring in physical education, and I taught swimming as one way to support myself, so I had taken teaching courses from the Red Cross and the YMCA. I had to leave school when the scholarship money ran out in my junior year.

What did you find most difficult about running the swim school in the beginning?
Learning how to gauge kids' skill levels and readiness to learn. At first I would take any child who came, but I soon began to realize some children weren't ready to swim. Another thing I found difficult was managing a staff and discovering the job couldn't be just fun and games. Sometimes you have to fire someone, and that's not very pleasant.

How did you come to be director of the swim school at Mission Bay?
I ran the Virginia swim school and worked as a coach for four years, but I didn't have the opportunity to run a large program—I could only do summer or afterschool hours. Then the head of the American Swim Coaches Association (the group that operates SwimAmerica) passed on an advertisement for a swim school director at Mission Bay. It's a fabulous training center with four pools and a diving well. I was scared that they wouldn't want me without a college degree, but I sent in my resume anyway. I was asked to come in for an interview, and I got the job.

What is your job like?
I manage a staff of five instructors during the winter, and in the summer I'll have between 15 and 20. My hours are from 8 A.M. to 4 P.M. Right now I'm doing a lot of paperwork to set up the swim school—advertising, program development, planning a seasonal bulletin board. One hour

a day I coach the top swimmers, the kids who want to go on to a swim team. I do all the stroke work with the advanced children, which is fun because they are competent swimmers honing their skills. I take them to meets and do social activities as well.

What do you like most about your work?

I've always enjoyed children and have a facility for teaching. It's so rewarding to teach kids how to swim. You're really helping them to learn a skill they will use for the rest of their lives. It's fun to think that 700 children went through my Virginia program and learned to swim. Here in Florida, where there's a drowning every week—there are canals everywhere and many people have backyard pools—I feel I'm doing a community service by teaching kids to swim.

Are there any drawbacks to your job?

In the beginning, when I was strictly teaching, I always felt soggy and my hair was never dry. Now as a manager, I don't enjoy the hiring or firing process. You'd love to extend everyone a job, and saying "No" to someone is difficult, but it takes a very special kind of person to help children learn to swim.

What have your proudest achievements been over the last five years?

Getting this job was a dream—more than that, because I never even knew I could do this as a full-time job. In general, you get such a rush when a child who doesn't catch on for weeks or months finally does. It's fun to share in children's excitement and achievements.

What advice would you give to someone considering a career as a swim instructor for children?

For one thing, earn your credentials. Find a SwimAmerica swim school and take the training. When you've developed enough expertise, you can apply for a directorship and eventually run your own swim school. There are coaches all over the country who need knowledgeable swim school directors who know the technical side of swimming. Do some volunteer teaching, if possible, and read some basic parenting and child care books to gain an understanding about how kids of different ages develop. You need to know where the child is developmentally to teach on their level. Work as an aid in a nursery school to develop some leadership skills.

Gus F. Pernetz, 24,
ski instructor and coach,
Vail and Beaver Creek,
Vail, Colorado
Years in the field: seven

How did you get started as a ski instructor?
I was going to college in Vermont and racing for the school. I was on the mountain a lot, so I started working part time with the local ski school.

What was that first job like?
On weekends I taught mostly children just getting started in skiing. Because I was a pretty good skier, I sometimes worked with the more advanced kids. Usually if I had a class on Saturday I'd have the same kids on Sunday. It was a family resort, so during Christmas and school breaks I would stay and work to make money.

Is it typical to begin as a part-timer?
Yes. If you live close to a resort, you can start teaching part time in high school. Most likely if you're in school you'll start out working with younger kids.

What was hardest thing about teaching in the beginning?
Having the confidence to be able to perform under pressure. Your supervisors and peers are always watching over you. Also there was the fear of failing—you want the kids to reach certain levels of ability. If they don't, you feel it's your fault.

How did you come to work in Colorado?
I went to school for resort management, and to finish I needed to do some management training. I came out here to do it but the program wasn't really what I wanted, so I decided to work for the ski school rather than go on and get

my degree. I enjoyed teaching and the people out here. I also saw growth in it. Now I'm fully certified through the Professional Skier's Association. It's a national program that offers three levels of training and testing. It was almost like going back to school—I had to take tests, write essays and demonstrate my skills.

What kind of growth did you see for someone who was an instructor?

When I was working part-time in Vermont, I really didn't see any growth, but out here in Vail there are a lot of opportunities to grow within the sport. The direction I'm taking is coaching. Within the next ten years I'd like to coach a regional or a national team—teens and others competing worldwide.

What is your workweek like?

I teach and coach full time—seven days a week during ski season, which lasts from November through April. Most days I'm on the slopes from about 8:30 in the morning until 3:30 in the afternoon. Two days a week I coach high-level skiers who go to the local high school; the other three weekdays I teach kids who are on vacation. On weekends I work with a development team—kids who want to race. Usually the caliber of the kids I teach is quite high, and many of the ones who come during holidays are returning clients. Since this is my fifth year working here I've had the opportunity to see kids grow. It's quite exciting.

After work I often hang out with the other instructors for awhile and we chat about how our day was. Then I work out in the gym. That's important because I'm skiing most of the day, and since I have a lot of teens, I'm doing a lot of high-energy skiing. I have to stay in shape so that I have the strength and stamina I need. Working out is also my way to unwind.

Do you feel you have an impact on the kids you teach beyond their learning the sport?

You're not just a ski instructor, you're a role model. You're helping kids to be more aggressive and disciplined, not only as skiers but in all areas of their lives. Often in the beginning they are shy and don't communicate well with other kids. When they start learning more, their attitude changes and you see them become more outgoing and talkative. You see them feel more powerful, and that can help them in school and in life.

Are there are other aspects of the job you enjoy?
I enjoy the responsibility and feeling that people can depend on me. We instructors are pros, and we put a lot of time and training into our work. We always give 110 percent. I love it everyday I'm out there—being able to look at the sky and out at the mountain range is incredible.

Is there anything you don't like about your job?
I wish the money were better. Since this is a seasonal job, the hard part is at the end of the season when you have to figure out your plans for the summer. The off season for me is from May to October, and in the past I've worked as a mountain guide and led bike tours in the area. Another option is to teach outside of the country during the off season. I'd like to coach some regional teams in South America or New Zealand maybe.

What advice can you offer to a high school student who is interested in becoming a ski instructor?
If you're going to teach kids, you really have to be responsible. Avoid the ski resort attitude of going out every night and drinking. Start by teaching part time on weekends and maybe get involved working at a nursery school or in a Big Brother program. You have to be able to understand and deal with different personalities and to be able to act according to the situation, so it might help to work toward an associate degree in psychology. And you need to know how to ski, and have some training in how to teach the sport.

Rudy Van Daele, 37,
owner and director,
Life Sport, Inc.,
New York, New York
Years in the field: 15

How did you get your start teaching gymnastics?
I was a junior in high school and on the gymnastics team.

My younger sister was a freshman and she started to do gymnastics, so I assisted her coach. Later, I helped coach the women's team at the college I was attending and was recommended to coach at some local gymnastics schools. In college I studied theater, sculpture and physical education, but I wasn't interested in getting a specific degree. By then I was heavily involved with sculpture but continued with gymnastics. I went to the gym a minimum of four days a week, three hours a day. I always did my own workouts, but I also coached the girl's gymnastics team at Queen's College as well as a program called progressive gymnastics at a privately owned children's gym.

What led you to settle on teaching gymnastics as a career?

I came to Manhattan to exhibit my sculpture, and while I was there a friend asked if I would cover a gymnastics class on the West Side. I did, and after that they kept on asking for me. I did this for five years while still sculpting, but I no longer had time to exhibit my work: All my attention became focused on teaching. I left when someone new took over the gym and began some business practices that made me uncomfortable. Leaving was emotional—the children and parents contacted me and offered to help me start up my own place. I call it Life Sport because the connotation is that this is something you begin at any age, and once you begin you can always continue.

What helped prepare you for teaching gymnastics to children?

For one thing, experience: I've been personally involved in gymnastics since I was about ten when my brother, who's two years older than me, began teaching me. I also feel that experiences in school and the way I was raised have a lot to do with how I relate to kids now. After grammar school and high school, I became very interested in education. I felt that in school kids were not given the ability to understand themselves and were just being filled up with information.

As an athlete I was popular in high school, and I came to realize that I could help make someone who wasn't very popular become so in his or her own right. And I come from a close and affectionate family. I believe that's the key to how I teach. The most obvious thing to do when teaching is to pay attention to the child.

What did you find difficult about teaching kids in the beginning?

The difficulties are that a lot of kids are affected by things in their lives. Sometimes it's hard to get past that to make contact with who the child is. Also, every kid fidgets in a new situation. This may be normal, but it's not productive. If you tell them to please pay attention, they've heard it all before and won't respond. You have to make it interesting. First you have to learn something about each child. I tell them, "You're the coach and I'm the student." That way they teach me about themselves.

As a coach, there's nothing that's that difficult because when you take on the role of coach, you have an obligation to maintain a professional relationship with children. That means you're there for them. You should work with a large variety of kids; each one—even those with learning disabilities, Down's syndrome, physical anomalies.

Tell me about your business.

Mostly these are afterschool programs that take place between 2:30 and 7:30 P.M. Life Sport has an enrollment of approximately 500 students, ages two and up. I operate everything in the business except bookkeeping and accounting. There are approximately 11 coaches. This program has attracted such diverse instructors as former Olympic coaches and Broadway choreographers.

What do you like most?

As a coach, you help shape a child's achievements, but it has to be the child's excitement; it is his or her accomplishment. I like the continuity of teaching the same children year after year. I have students who are now in their twenties who remember ideas we discussed when they were four. A relationship between a coach and a gymnast becomes a family one—kids want you to be part of their life, come over for dinner, see their room. Teaching kids is a poetic thing to do. In teaching, you've got a delicate relationship with another person. Spontaneous hugging is the best. I will always want this personal contact with the kids.

What advice would you give to someone still in high school who is thinking of coaching children's gymnastics?

First, spend some time in a gym and make sure you like the atmosphere and the contact with the people there. Assist a teacher to see if you have a talent for coaching. Think about where you'd like to do this. It gets very involved and takes a good amount of time to become proficient. You need to know the technical aspects of the sport as well as have a deep affection for children. USGF (United States Gymnastics Federation) certification is advisable. And you should remember that while you can make a decent living at this, most of what you'll get is the satisfaction of working with other people.

If you have never outgrown your delight in dolls, the thrill of sending a toy train chugging 'round a minimountain or the sheer fun of playing children's board games, you are a natural to work in a toy store. Not as a cashier in a chain, but as a salesperson in a smaller toy or hobby store that specializes in top-of-the-line and educational toys or collectibles.

magine getting paid to work in a room filled with shelves of games and puzzles, building blocks and books, fire trucks and stuffed animals. One of your jobs may be to assemble a miniature barnyard, space station or dollhouse. Or you may be asked to play the role of Noah and line up pairs of animals at the entrance to an ark. Working in a toy store can be as magical a job as being one of Santa's elves. You're surrounded with things from your childhood and have the opportunity to

41

direct your passion for playthings into a job and even into a career.

Customers who want more than a perfunctory point to aisle seven when they ask where toys for preschoolers are prefer mom-and-pop- type toy and hobby stores over large chain discount stores. They appreciate personalized service from friendly salespeople. If they're happy with what they buy, they will usually come back birthday after birthday, holiday after holiday.

In addition to an interest in toys, you need a keen business sense and a knack for sales to succeed. A salesperson's job involves recommending just the right toy to customers who may be perplexed parents, or, more likely, childless relatives. If you work in a hobby store, you may be asked to help complete an elaborate model airplane or offer pointers on getting a remote-control sailboat to work.

Good salespeople can rattle off the contents of a toy barnyard, and easily assemble multipiece playthings. And, like all good salespeople, they are friendly, but not pushy, helpful without being overbearing. They make it their business to read toy manufacturers' catalogs and to actually play with the merchandise when time allows, so that they can talk about or demonstrate what a particular toy does.

They are interested in the role toys play in the growth of children, and they can talk knowledgeably about which toys are safe and appropriate for tykes of all ages. Hobby store employees often are personally involved in their store's specialty, whether it's trains, cars or military miniatures.

Because they are employed by small businesses, salespeople's responsibilities include the range of tasks that running a small store involves: taking inventory, operating the cash register, wrapping gifts, arranging merchandise and tidying the premises.

Some toy store salespeople who have mastered the mechanics of running a store go on to open their own businesses. Most do so after working for a number of years, perhaps moving up to become a manager of a store before striking out on their own. Wherever this career takes you, there's one guarantee: Going to work each day will feel more like going out to play.

What You Need to Know

Toy and hobby store salespeople gain most of their knowledge on the job, but it may help to have a sense of the following:

❏ How children develop at different ages in terms of physical strength, verbal skills and manual dexterity

❏ What types of toys appeal most to kids of various ages

❏ Knowledge of and experience using the hobby materials in a specialty store

Necessary Skills

❏ How to run a cash register, make change, process a credit card

❏ How to wrap a gift (helpful)

❏ Ability to assemble toys with small and/or many pieces

❏ Good memorization skills (so you can easily locate products for customers)

❏ Ability to communicate well with customers and share with your managers what customers tell you

Do You Have What It Takes?

❏ A sensitivity to customers' needs; an intuitiveness that helps you determine what someone is looking for even if they can't verbalize it well

❏ The ability to handle customer complaints without losing your temper and to let such situations roll off your back

❏ Patience, which comes in handy when customers can't make up their minds and tie you up for long periods without buying

❏ A cheerful, friendly disposition

❏ Punctuality (especially important in a small store)

❏ Ability to take direction from store owner or manager

❏ A knack for communicating with kids (besides dealing with parents, you will probably talk to the children who come into the store, asking them which toys they like best and why)

Physical Attributes

❏ Well-groomed appearance
❏ Physical stamina (you'll be on your feet most of the day, sometimes lifting heavy items)

Education

A high school diploma or equivalent is helpful but not required.

Licenses Required

None

Job Outlook

Competition for jobs: very competitive

There are fewer than 2,000 toy stores in the country (not counting large self-service chains, which do not require that employees have any special interest in or knowledge about toys). There are 4,000 to 5,000 specialty hobby shops throughout the United States. Many employees of both toy and hobby stores, however, are part-timers or high school students who leave after a short while. This level of turnover may make it somewhat easier for someone with a commitment to the field to land a full-time sales job.

The Ground Floor

Entry-level job: sales clerk

On-the-Job Responsibilities

Beginners

❏ Assist customers (explain and demonstrate how different toys are used, make purchase suggestions, point out where certain items are located)
❏ Keep an eye on children in the store, perhaps asking them which toys they like best and so forth, to get an

idea of what's hot among kids
- ❏ Handle customer purchases, exchanges or refunds at cash register
- ❏ Wrap purchases bought as gifts
- ❏ Assemble complicated toys for customers
- ❏ Keep store neat and tidy
- ❏ Unpack and arrange new merchandise attractively on shelves
- ❏ Tag toys with prices and later, markdowns
- ❏ Help out with end-of-year inventory

Managers

In addition to the above:
- ❏ Schedule employees' weekly hours; find substitutes or fill in for clerks who are unable to work
- ❏ Order merchandise (sometimes)
- ❏ Handle customer problems that salesperson cannot resolve
- ❏ Train and supervise salespeople
- ❏ Motivate staff to make sales quotas

Owners

- ❏ Hire and fire employees
- ❏ Study toy catalogs and determine which merchandise to have in stock
- ❏ Order new merchandise
- ❏ Keep track of inventory and reorders from manufacturers
- ❏ Manage the books—either alone or with the help of an outside accountant
- ❏ Develop and carry out advertising strategies and promotions
- ❏ Design and direct store window displays
- ❏ Attend local, national and even international toy fairs and hobby shows

When You'll Work

Work hours vary. Some stores open late and close relatively early—from, say, 10 A.M. to 6 P.M.—and full-time staff would be expected to work the entire eight hours. It's not unusual for a store to have evening hours at least once a week. From Thanksgiving to Christmas most toy stores extend their hours, in which case employees may work eight-hour shifts or longer. Most stores are open on Saturday; some even open for five hours on Sunday.

Time Off

How much vacation time you get depends on the generosity of the store owner. Beginners on a part-time schedule will not get the same consideration as long-term, full-time workers when it comes to taking time off. Most stores also restrict vacation time during the peak holiday sales season—from Thanksgiving until the beginning of January.

Perks

❑ First peek at the latest toys
❑ Discounts on merchandise (how much may vary according to whether you're full time or part time)

Who's Hiring

❑ Specialty toy stores
❑ Hobby shops

Places You'll Go

Beginners: No travel potential
Managers and owners: Occasional travel
Store owners and managers usually attend the annual Toy Fair sponsored by the Toy Manufacturers of America (TMA) in New York, as well as regional shows also sponsored by the TMA. The store owner who wants to offer more than what's available domestically may go to international toy fairs. Hobby store owners and managers often attend an annual show sponsored by the Radio-Controlled Hobby Trade Association as well as regional shows that focus on individual hobbies.

Surroundings

The store may be large and spacious, with fancy fixtures (such as an elaborate desk for the cash register) and attractive shelving, or it may be small and cluttered, like a toddler's playroom. In many stores, certain toys are set out for display and for the children of customers to play with while the grown-ups browse. Stores may be located in large shopping malls, along shopping strips, or they may be freestanding.

Starting pay for most sales clerks is little more than the minimum wage in the area; with experience, clerks may receive a small raise. Some companies add incentives—a commission or percentage on each sale, a percentage above any quotas that may be set or added merchandise discounts. Store managers, with their increased responsibilities, usually are paid a yearly salary competitive with that of other retail managers in the region. Store owners bring home whatever is left of the year's profits after paying employees, overhead, insurance and the cost of new merchandise.

◆ **Dollars and Cents**

Enthusiastic and motivated sales clerks who consistently sell well and go out of their way to learn everything they can about the toys and the business may very likely be promoted to store manager. How quickly a clerk makes this step up depends in part on when there is an opening for a manager in the store. Employees who wish to go on to buy their own business would do well to take some accounting courses at a community college and to learn all they can from their employer regarding the ins and the outs of being a store owner—how much money they will need to get started, how to deal with toy suppliers and to establish credit with them, etc.

◆ **Moving Up**

Jobs exist wherever there are toy and hobby stores, which can be found everywhere from major metropolitan areas to small towns.

◆ **Where the Jobs Are**

The Male/Female Equation

Women gravitate toward work in a toy store more than men do—perhaps because they are more likely to have had extensive contact with kids and therefore to have developed an interest in toys.

Making Your Decision: What to Consider

The Bad News

- Low hourly wage for employees; owners' incomes suffer when economy is bad
- Long hours and slow time when store is not busy
- Routine tasks, including cleaning store
- No sure path to advancement

The Good News

- Employees usually get discounts on merchandise
- Work environment is fun
- Plenty of opportunities to meet new people, interact with kids, play with toys
- Great training ground if you someday want to own your own store

More Information Please

There are no professional organizations for toy store employees and owners. New business owners may want to contact their chamber of commerce and local merchant's association, both of which may provide helpful information for starting and running a business in the area as well as provide informal networking opportunities. Toy store owners should also contact the Toy Manufacturers of America (see below); the TMA sponsors regional toy shows as well as the New York Toy Fair each February, to which retailers are invited.

Toy Manufacturers of America
200 Fifth Avenue
New York, New York 10010
212-675-1141

Jackie S. Ernst, 24,
retail sales manager
Scarsdale Childs Play,
Scarsdale, New York
Years in the business: three

How did you get started?
My mother owns the store. I was working as a dental assistant when she asked if I could come in and work part time during the Christmas crunch.

Do you think part-time is a good way to ease into toy selling?
I think it's the best way to go. You ease into it bit by bit. I know that personally I needed time to get into the swing of things, for instance, to observe my mother's sales technique.

What swayed you to stay on full-time?
It was a good feeling when people would come in and depend on me to help them find just the right gift for a particular child. Customers know me by name, I know them by name, and I like that closeness with the public. Besides, as a dental assistant I knew I was never going to have some-

thing of my own. Working here I know I'll eventually take over the store or be otherwise involved in the business.

Your title is manager. What are your responsibilities?
My title is manager because there has to be one. I oversee the other employees, but we all basically do the same job and each of us works just as hard as the others. I sell, help buy toys, enhance customer relations. We keep a big book of things customers request and when the toys come in, we call the person who wanted it.

At the end of the day we're so tired and beat it's too much to stay and clean up the store. So in the morning we all pitch in and straighten up. The only difference between me and the other salespeople here is that when a customer comes in with a problem or to return a toy, I'm the one they deal with.

How have you become familiar with toys and children? Did growing up around the store help?
I was 14 when my mother opened this toy store, so I didn't really grow up with it. A lot of what I know now I've learned from customers. They come in and tell us which toys are great and which ones aren't so great. I also go to the toy fair (in New York) with my mom; since she's been in the business for 11 years she knows everybody. You learn as you go. As you sell toys you learn what to sell. Most of the toys have labels saying which ages they're appropriate for. That's a good guide in the beginning. We allow kids to play with whatever is in the store; you can get a pretty good sense of what children of different ages are interested in just by watching. Sometimes we'll have customers come in and say they've seen a particular item and often we'll order it.

Is there anything about your job you don't like?
The time right after Christmas when the store is very quiet. I love when people are buying things and I hear the cash register open four hundred times a day.

What do you find most difficult about your job?
It takes a lot of work to sell. Customers aren't always happy, merchandise doesn't always come in on time, and people don't see that that's not your fault. But it's a fun

business. Who wouldn't like it? There are parts that people don't see. When we go to do the buying at the toy fair we play with everything we buy. In the showrooms they have all the stuff out and we play with it there, too. Mom travels far and wide to find the best toys; she goes to California and to Nuremburg, Germany, for instance.

What makes working in a small, specialty shop like yours different from, say, running the cash register in a big chain toy store?

People come to this type of store for the personalized service. We work with each customer individually to help them find the toy they want, then we wrap it and put a card on it and they're ready to go to the birthday party or wherever. We have people who call from their car phone because they can't get a parking spot, asking for a certain toy and asking us to wrap it up and bring it out. And we do.

During the summer we do a big sleep-away camp business. Parents send out care packages to their kids at camp; they'll come in at the beginning of the summer, pick out a bunch of stuff and then leave it to us to divide up the loot into several small packages and send them out once a week or so. We once had a father all the way from Chicago call because he'd heard we were the store that did such great care packages.

Where could a job like yours lead?

Obviously a toy store employee could eventually have his or her own business. One of my favorite parts is doing the buying, seeing what's new. I think I would like to become a sales rep for a toy manufacturer someday. I like the idea of going on the road. Sometimes in the store I feel a little stuck.

What advice can you offer to someone who's contemplating working in a toy store?

Get in there and just do it. You could go to school for retail management for as long as you want, but the job won't be anything like what you'd expect when you go into it. It has to be something you have a knack for. It's a tough business, dealing with the public. There are all different kinds of people, and you often have to change your personality to communicate well with each one.

Pam Rinderknecht, 36,
owner, No More Monkey Business,
The Woodlands, Texas
Years in business: six

How did you get started in the toy business?
My daughter was taking gymnastics with the son of No
More Monkey Business's former owner. One day, while
the kids were in class, we had a chance to chat about the
store and my interest in children's books. She asked if I
would like to work for her. We got along well and had a lot
of the same ideas and philosophies about running a business
and what we would want to provide for parents and kids.

What sorts of things did you do in the beginning?
I started as a sales clerk. Besides helping customers, I spent
a lot of time going through toy manufacturers' catalogs
with the owner and telling her what I thought of the merchandise. Together we did a lot of moving things around to
make certain all the toys were visible to customers. I took a
lot of initiative, but she never told me I was out of bounds.
For instance, when I went into other stores, I would write
down the name of merchandise and books that would fit in
our store, then call and ask for catalogs. We expanded our
range of merchandise that way. After about six months I
was promoted to manager. The main difference in that position was that I took on more responsibilities as far as doing
payroll and ordering merchandise on my own, especially
books.

How did you come to own the store?
Again, it was circumstantial. The owner wanted to have
another child and was moving into a new house. The lease
for the store was coming up and she had decided to close it
because it would have been too much with everything else
going on her life. I talked to her about possibly buying it.
She warned me that being a store owner is not easy. And I
had seen what it was like—it's a long road. But I didn't
want to see the store close, so I bought the business.

Did you make any major changes once you took over?
I decided to concentrate on what I was selling. A lot of

items in that store were higher-end items, but our number one business is selling birthday gifts—which most people don't want to spend a lot on. We also had a lot of teachers' supplies in stock, but they weren't really moving; I got rid of them. So I did take the store in a different direction: I got the average price of the toys down to where most were affordable birthday gifts, and I also increased the number of books in the store.

What kind of preparation did you have for running a toy store?

When I was in high school I worked as a sales clerk in a grocery store, so I knew how to run a cash register. I had also worked in a department store when I was first married. And I took a business course in high school, though at the time I never thought I'd ever go into business for myself. But the one thing I found I have is good business sense—an instinct for what will work.

Was this experience enough to go on at first?

I definitely didn't know everything I needed to know when I bought the store. For the most part I ran the store by the seat of my pants. I just did what I felt was right. And I found there needed to be a balance between that and good business sense. If I could have done anything differently I might have started learning about accounting and the nuts and bolts of running a business sooner. After I'd owned the store for a year I took an accounting course and decided I needed an accountant—someone who could handle the paperwork for me. I probably went for a year after that without understanding the balance sheets he was sending me.

Finally, when I had someone show me what everything meant and what I needed to do it began to make sense and I could see what I would need to do to make the business work. For instance, I went for a couple of years without advertising and finally decided I would have to do something to boost sales. So I put a commercial on the local cable TV station and my sales that year jumped 48 percent. This year I'm doing a catalog through a Dallas-based business. They weren't cheap. But the business needed a shot in the arm and my sales have really been up as a result.

What have you found most difficult as a toy store owner?

Not having enough time to do everything I want to do. I've had to give up some things by hiring another manager. I have her do the payroll, the time sheets and some of the ordering. It's hard: You have to trust someone else to do things right, even if they don't do it exactly the way you do.

How many employees do you have?

I have four, and I'm in the store full-time now.

What do you enjoy most?

I get to meet people every day. And we're doing something different every day. We can be as creative as we want to be. The freedom to do what I want to appeals to me. My decisions are mine, and I don't have to ask anyone else. I have very definite ideas about what I want to do and what directions I want to go in.

What would you change about the business?

The pay. I make very little for the amount of time I spend working; I put most of my profits back into the business. And sometimes I wonder why I've done what I've done, because it is an awful lot of work. I'll lie awake and think it's not worth it. Then someone will come running into the store and ask for a gift for a six year old, and I'll pick something that's just right and the customer will say she's really glad I'm here. Knowing that people appreciate me makes it worthwhile. People want toys they feel are good for their kids and not a pieces of junk. It's nice to feel I'm doing a service.

What personality traits do you think are essential for someone in this business?

Patience. We have people who let their kids do some awful things in the store. It takes a lot of tact to deal with that as well. You need to be friendly and sensitive to what people want.

What advice would you give to a young person contemplating the toy business?

Work as a clerk and learn the business from the ground up. It takes a pretty strong person to go into something they know nothing about. I guess the other thing would be to ask questions of anyone who's been in the business. I went in thinking I knew a lot and found out that I didn't. Take business courses for a good base and understanding of the fundamentals so you get a real handle on what you're doing.

Brian Herrington, 21,
sales clerk, Toys and Co.,
Greensboro, North Carolina
Years in the business: two

How did you get interested in selling toys?
I've always been a kid at heart and have a tendency to be a person who dislikes a lot of stress. Kids are probably some of the best friends you can ever have. You can play with them and they don't really care who you are or anything. They just want to have fun—no stress. I like making kids happy, and toys are a primary component of happiness for children.

Is this your first job selling toys?
Yes. I was working for an accounting firm and then went into the Army Reserve for training. When I got back my accounting job was terminated. I called a couple friends and one who was working here said that they might be accepting applications. So I dropped by, filled out an application and started the next day.

Did you have to go through any sort of training?
Dolls are probably about 70 percent of the sales here, so there was a lot of memorization of dolls. You have to know thousands of names, thirty different artists, where the dolls are made, and, if they're limited editions, how many were made. And this changes every year. I had to learn how to do inventory for the store, how to check in stock when it gets shipped in. I had to learn all kinds of stuff on the cash register, like what codes to use for what categories of toys. I also had to learn to use the machine that verifies credit card status.

What's your favorite part of the job?
When we get some kids in and their mom and dad leaves

them at the play tables to go look around the store. I'll go to the play tables, play with the kids and find out what they like. My theory is you don't have to sell the parents—you have to sell the kids on the toy and then they'll sell the parents.

What kind preparation did you have for this job?
I used to teach a swim clinic for little kids at a country club. I was responsible for ten kids for an hour and a half, and we had the best time. I believe that if you like what you're doing, you have a tendency to be really good at it.

The only other sales experience I've had was at a video rental place. That job made me realize how serious people get about shopping and spending money. I think that what really turned me on to toys, or kids, is that working with them is a little less tense than working with adult customers.

Is there anything about your job you don't particularly like?
No, not really. I've had some hard days, but I don't think I would still be here after two years if I didn't enjoy it.

What have been some of the hard things?
You get some real losers working in retail sometimes. There have been a few here who have been lazy, and I have had to pick up their slack. And I've dealt with a few irate customers, but not many. I take it with a grain of salt. You can't please everybody.

What would you advise someone in high school to do to prepare for this type of work?
It's all in the attitude. I would tell them to stay young, think of yourself as a kid. The people at the top—the store managers and owners—can teach you a lot. I think people who are education majors take stuff like this a little too seriously. I probably got trained the best way—I learned it from the parents and the kids.

If your favorite childhood game was setting up a classroom with your dolls, working in a real classroom might be just the career for you. As a preschool teacher or a teacher aide you will be interacting almost exclusively with pint-sized people. You'll help ease them into the world of discipline and social interaction and give them a sense of how much fun learning can be.

Preschool teachers decide what activities their fledgling students will do each day and when. They come up with arts and crafts projects, lead the children in group activities such as singing songs or playing games, plan and serve snacks, read aloud and supervise outdoor play. After class they keep up to date on the latest in children's literature and music; in addition, they may have conferences with the

59

parents of students to discuss the children's behavior and progress.

Teacher aides, sometimes called teacher assistants, paraeducators or education paraprofessionals, usually work in kindergartens and elementary schools, though some junior high and high schools employ them. Some of these jobs are purely clerical—handing out papers, making copies of handouts, collecting lunch money or grading papers. Others involve more teaching and interacting directly with children, helping them to master reading or math skills, supervising the decoration of a bulletin board or leading a learning game. Some teacher aides get a degree so that they can become certified teachers.

Whatever the long-term goals of the teacher aide, it's what she brings to the classroom each day that matters most. Her presence frees up the instructor so that she has more time to focus on the demands of teaching. The aide keeps the classroom in good running order and well stocked with essentials. She is there to help discipline the kids when necessary, and in many cases to help reinforce the lessons by working individually with children.

As an educator, whether you are at the head of the class or second in command, you represent one more caring adult in the lives of your students. To be successful it's essential to feel comfortable with children, have great patience and be able to talk to kids in ways they can understand.

The best preschool teachers and teacher aides are able to motivate kids and to pique their interest in the lesson at hand. They can bring order to an unruly class without resorting to yelling or scare tactics. They can sympathize with the short attention span of a four year old or the moodiness of a twelve year old. In short, a love of youngsters is far more important to a job well done than extensive knowledge of a particular subject matter.

There are some intriguing benefits to the profession as well. For instance, employees in most schools finish work in the mid-afternoon and have great vacation schedules—summers and many holidays off and a long Christmas break. If these advantages appeal to you, and if you derive particular pleasure from seeing a little face light up when a new concept finally kicks in, then you're probably well suited to work in the classroom.

What You Need to Know

- ❏ How a school is organized and operates
- ❏ Basics of reading, writing, mathematics, science, grammar and other subjects taught in your classroom
- ❏ The physical, social, emotional and intellectual stages of development of children of different ages
- ❏ Games, songs, crafts and other activities that are age appropriate

Necessary Skills

- ❏ How to communicate information to children in ways that they can understand and absorb through the use of examples, stories and group discussion
- ❏ How to make up lesson plans and schedules (pre-school teachers)
- ❏ How to conduct group activities—singing songs, playing word games and so forth
- ❏ How to prepare instructional materials for distribution or display in the classroom
- ❏ Clerical abilities such as filing, record keeping (of grades, attendance, health records), using office equipment such as copy machines (teacher aide)
- ❏ How to grade tests and check homework (teacher aide)
- ❏ How to operate audiovisual and other equipment often used in classrooms
- ❏ Ability to monitor and discipline groups of children in the classroom, at lunch or on the playground

Do You Have What It Takes?

- ❏ A love of kids
- ❏ Resourcefulness (the ability to come up with new ways of presenting difficult material)
- ❏ Cheerful demeanor
- ❏ Ability to get along with and take direction from the teacher or director, who may be younger or have less

◆ **Getting Into the Field**

experience working with children than you do
- ❏ Initiative (the self-confidence to see what needs to be done in a classroom without always waiting for instructions from the teacher or director)
- ❏ Patience
- ❏ A sense of fairness, which comes in handy when dealing with tiffs among children or when assigning kids special responsibilities (for instance, making sure all children get a chance to be room monitor)
- ❏ A good sense of humor (to get you through the day)

Physical Attributes

- ❏ Stamina (much of the day will be spent on your feet bending over desks and tables and in motion)
- ❏ Good personal hygiene (you will be working closely with others and need to set a good example)

Education

High school diploma or graduate equivalency diploma (GED) necessary for those who want to become a teacher aide.

The requirements for teachers in preschools vary from state to state—from nothing but on-the-job training to an associate degree in early childhood education, to a four-year bachelor's degree. To find out exactly what a particular state requires of preschool teachers check with the department of social services or a local child care and referral agency. A CDA (Child Development Associate) accreditation is recognized by all states except Indiana as being helpful in securing a preschool teaching position.

Licenses Required

As many as 15 states currently certify or license teacher aides. The requirements for certification vary widely from state to state and may include anything from 30 credit hours of college to a year or two of practical classroom experience. Aides working in special education need paraprofessional permits in Kansas, Texas and Wisconsin; these permits are acquired in different ways. For instance, in Kansas the state pays for and provides in-service training for teacher aides in special education.

Job prospects: very good
The employment of preschool workers (of whom preschool teachers are one group) is expected to increase 50 percent between now and the year 2005 according to the Bureau of Labor Statistics. The growth in the number of jobs reflects the growing number of young children who will need care and a shift in the type of child care arrangements parents use.

Employment of teacher aides is also expected to grow faster than average, reflecting rising school enrollments and a greater use of aides.

Entry-level job: preschool teacher, teacher aide or assistant

◆ Job Outlook

◆ The Ground Floor

◆ On-the-Job Responsibilities

Preschool Teachers

❏ Plan in advance what each day's lessons and activities will be
❏ Lead children in group activities—songs, learning games and storytelling
❏ Help individual children use materials and toys
❏ Plan and supervise small field trips (i.e. to the local fire station or library)
❏ Prepare and serve snacks
❏ Assist children with hand washing, shoe tying, taking off and putting on sweaters, coats, mittens, hats, etc.
❏ Read stories aloud
❏ Discipline children when necessary
❏ Keep classroom bright and cheerful; decorate bulletin boards according to season or theme

❏ If an aide is present, delegate responsibilities

❏ Discuss children's behavior and progress with parents

❏ Outside of class, keep up with the latest in kid's literature and music

❏ Read magazine articles and books about child behavior, development and education to keep abreast of new ideas

Beginners and Experienced Teacher Aides

❏ Take role call, collect lunch money, grade tests and record the scores, copy handouts and other classroom "office work"

❏ Set up and operate audiovisual equipment

❏ Keep classroom well stocked with paper, pencils, crayons, notebooks, arts and crafts supplies

❏ Keep room tidy

❏ Decorate bulletin boards and classroom walls

❏ Take charge of the classroom while the teacher is absent

❏ Supervise children on the playground, in the library or in the cafeteria

❏ Prepare materials for lessons determined by the teacher

❏ Review with students material already presented by the teacher

❏ Work with students in small groups or individually, tutoring them on specific subjects or working on craft projects

❏ Give parents progress and behavior reports (sometimes)

When You'll Work

Both preschool workers and teacher aides may work full time five days a week for seven and a half hours per day. Some preschools have more limited hours (three to five hours a day); some teacher aides work only part time. Teachers and aides usually come in a week before school starts in the fall to set up the classroom and they stay for a week after school lets out in the summer to close things down.

Vacation days correspond to school breaks, including federal holidays, and usually two weeks off at Christmas and a one-week break during the spring. Generally, preschool teachers and aides have summers off, except in preschools that stay open for shorter hours and days during the summer, or in public schools that have adopted the new year-round program; in this case, teachers will have several two- or three-week long breaks throughout the year.

◆ **Time Off**

- ❏ Shorter than average work hours, with the day ending in the early afternoon
- ❏ Summers off
- ❏ Benefits, such as medical insurance, which continue during summer vacation
- ❏ Free entry to museums, zoos, cultural events and other typical field trip destinations
- ❏ Access to the school library and computer lab

◆ **Perks**

- ❏ Public and private nursery schools
- ❏ Public and private kindergartens and elementary schools (these account for 80 percent of teacher aide jobs)
- ❏ Montessori schools
- ❏ Church-affiliated schools
- ❏ Head Start programs
- ❏ Schools for "special" children—those with mental and/or physical disabilities, as well as gifted students

◆ **Who's Hiring**

Preschool teachers and teacher aides spend most of their time in the classroom, an environment that varies according to the age group and the school. Nursery schools and kindergartens are likely to be painted in cheerful colors and resemble Santa's workshop, since most are well stocked with educational toys. Public, inner-city schools

◆ **Surroundings**

have the highest student-teacher ratio, and their appearance can feel more like a fortress than a classroom; the equipment often leaves much to be desired as well.

Parent-supported public schools and private elementary schools (particularly those whose students pay hefty tuitions) sport the most pleasing environments and up-to-date equipment. At times, the classroom may be noisy as children engage in discussion, have free time or do arts and crafts projects; during lessons, study periods or rest periods the room will very likely be calm and quiet. Aides also spend time in the school cafeteria and library and on the playground. Most schools have private teachers' lounges where faculty can escape for a break from the classroom, a cup of coffee and some adult conversation.

Dollars and Cents

Pay varies according to region, work experience, level of education and job responsibilities. The average earnings for teacher aides is about $7.50 an hour. Paraprofessionals in urban areas, particularly in the Northeast, typically have the highest salaries in the profession. Pay is suspended during summer vacation, although medical insurance and other benefits continue.

Moving Up

There is no formal career ladder for preschool teachers and teacher aides: Advancement is defined by higher salary or increased responsibility. With further education in school administration a preschool teacher may move up to become director of a preschool. A minority of education paraprofessionals go on to obtain their teaching certificates, often by working as an assistant during the day and taking classes at night. Some school districts may even foot the bill for this, particularly ones in which there is a strong paraprofessional union.

Where the Jobs Are

Although there are job opportunities throughout the United States, preschool teachers and aides are most likely to find employment in regions that are experiencing increased enrollments. The South and the West have particularly fast-growing populations of preschoolers, kindergartners and elementary school-age kids.

The training of preschool teachers ranges from on-the-job experience to a year or more of college courses in early childhood education, which may be obtained from a university or community college. A Child Development Accreditation (CDA) is acquired with two years of classroom study and hands-on training; the credential is offered through:

The Council for Early Childhood Professional Recognition
1341 G Street, NW, Suite 400
Washington, D.C. 20005-3105
202-265-9090 or 800-424-4310

Most aides receive on-the-job training, which may include formal and informal instruction that covers operation of equipment, how to keep records and how to prepare instructional material.

◆ **Training**

The vast majority of teacher aides are women, although the ranks of male paraprofessionals are growing. Men can bring something special to the job, particularly in urban areas where many children come from single-parent families and do not have daily contact with male role models.

◆ **The Male/Female Equation**

◆ **Making Your Decision: What to Consider**

The Bad News

❏ Low salary; pay increases may be dictated by state and local education budgets
❏ No formal job advancement
❏ Much of the work may involve clerical duties
❏ Pay is suspended for two months during summer vacation

The Good News

❏ Generally excellent benefits, including paid vacations and medical insurance
❏ Some schools pay for aides to acquire continuing education that will lead to teacher certification
❏ Workday ends mid-afternoon; summers off

More Information Please

◆ American Montessori Society
150 Fifth Avenue, Suite 203
New York, New York 10011
212-924-3209

The society can provide listings of local AMS-affiliated schools and information on training programs and conferences.

American Federation of Teachers
Paraprofessionals and School-Related Personnel Division
555 New Jersey Avenue, NW
Washington, D.C. 20001
202-879-4400 or 800-238-1133

A public employees' union representing more than 100,000 education paraprofessionals across the country. AFT can provide information on training and certification opportunities, and it offers a quarterly newsletter for teacher assistants.

National Association for the Education of Young Children
1509 16th Street, N.W.
Washington, D.C. 20036
800-424-2460

The largest nonprofit professional organization for preschool teachers. Membership includes access to brochures, books and other information relevant to careers in early childhood education.

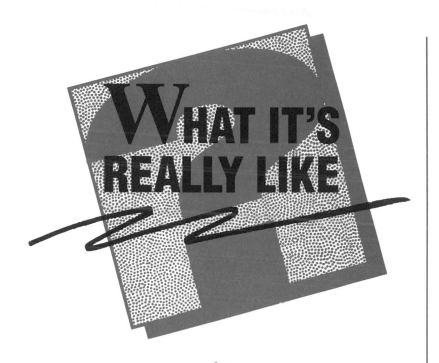

Tara W. Oliver, 33,
teacher assistant,
Bluford Communications Laboratory
Magnet School, Greensboro, North Carolina
Years in the field: 12

What prompted you to become a teacher's assistant?
Everyone in my family works in education, and ever since
I was little I wanted to be a teacher. It was always exciting
to me to see what children could do.

How many different jobs have you had in this field?
I've had two assistant jobs; I also worked as a receptionist
in the main office of the city schools for two years.

How did you get your first job?
I was working as a bank teller when one of the personnel
directors for city school employees came through the drive-
in window. I asked her to give me an interview; I told her I
was sure she would be impressed. So she did. After we
talked, she said she was going to mention my name to a
couple of principals. One of them called me in and I went
in twice on my lunch hour to see him. He created a position
for me in a kindergarten.

What did the job involve?
I worked for four kindergarten teachers. Each week I spent a whole day in each room, then on Fridays I spent an hour in each room. I took kids outside to play games, decorated bulletin boards, helped individual children learn basics like the alphabet. I also did some clerical stuff like running off papers. The rest of Friday I worked with the kids who were being rewarded for good behavior for the week by doing special fun activities.

This was a temporary position; after six months I got a permanent position in a third grade classroom. I loved third grade because you can do so much with children that age. I worked with the kids who needed special attention. That year we had all boys in our classroom. I think there were 23. Working with so many boys helped me learn how to have a structured classroom. It was fun; I really enjoyed it.

Where did you go from there?
The teacher I was working with switched schools and wanted me to go with her. I put in for a transfer, but someone with more seniority bumped me out. After that I got transferred to different schools five times until finally I got a permanent spot. The teacher I worked with was real energetic, and she gave me a lot of experience. Some teachers don't like assistants to work with children; they prefer to have them do more clerical things. Not mine. If she had a meeting to attend and they couldn't find a substitute, the teacher and principal felt comfortable leaving me there because they knew I could handle the kids.

Why did you leave the classroom to work as a receptionist?
I did that because I had just gotten married and wanted to work year-round. But I really missed the school. Every Friday I would go by and bring my kids a treat. Some of them would call me on the phone and ask me to come back and see them. After two and a half years I had a baby and thought I'd like to be able to have summers off again. I also missed the children. So I interviewed with four teachers here at Bluford who needed assistants, and I came back as a kindergarten teacher assistant.

What have your proudest accomplishments been since returning to the classroom?
Last year I was voted outstanding teacher assistant by the PTA. And I work on various committees at school. For instance, I bring in guest speakers for the entire school or just for my classroom. My evaluation since becoming an assistant has always been superior, even from principals.

What kind of training did you have?
None. When I got my first job, my oldest son was about three and raising him was all the experience I'd had. But my mother teaches special ed, I have two uncles who are school principals and an aunt who is a teacher. And my parents have always taught me to do the best you can and children will respond. If you show them you care, children are likely to succeed.

What is the hardest aspect of being a teacher assistant?
You have teachers with different personalities, and they all have different things they want you to do. Some make you feel right at home, and some let you know that this is *their* classroom. I've only had one teacher who was like that, and we got along fine after we had a sort of standoff: It was freezing outside one day when I was in charge of physical education, and I told the teacher it was too cold to go outside. She didn't like it but she accepted it.

What do you like most about what you're doing?
I'm working now with some kids who don't know the alphabet, numbers or colors. I love seeing them get excited when they accomplish something. I give them smiley faces on their papers, which they feel so proud of.

What do you like least?
I believe teacher assistants need more pay, at least those who give everything they have to their jobs.

Would you like to be in charge of the classroom some day?
Yes. In fact, I'm going back to school right now. Soon I'm going to transfer to a college that will allow me to earn my elementary education degree while working full time in school. I'll go at night, two classes a night, three nights a week. I'll be through in about two years.

What advice would you give to a young person contemplating a career as a teacher assistant?

You need to get experience working with children. Work as a babysitter or in a day care center or volunteer to tutor—anything that will allow you work with children of different ages and different abilities.

Leonard Edmonds, 43,
classroom assistant,
Conroy Education Center,
Pittsburgh, Pennsylvania
Years in field: 19

How did you get started?

I was working in a community day care center and was laid off. This was the year the Right to Education Law came into effect, so to comply the school districts went to the community centers to find classroom assistants. I was hired as an assistant here at Conroy, a school for the mentally disabled. My plan was to be here only for a year.

What kept you going?

Initially I liked the hours. My day started at 7:30 A.M. and was over at 3:00 P.M. As time progressed, I realized I enjoyed education and teaching. I'm a musician, and at one time I wanted to be a music teacher. And I've always loved kids. The money wasn't really that great so I always had two jobs, but between the two I made do. But the most important thing was that I came to see how essential teacher assistants are in education. Paraprofessionals, as we sometimes call ourselves, enable the professionals to be *more* professional.

Describe what you do.

I work in an autistic support class. There are eight kids, ages seven to ten. There is another assistant in the class, and the teacher and the two of us work as team. Specifically, I help with discipline and instruction, although I don't introduce new lessons.

Did you receive any special training to work as a teacher assistant?

There was no training provided by our district at the time I was hired. It was learn as you go. Now we have yearly conferences for paraprofessionals and workshops as well, and through our union we have initiated a paraprofessional training program.

What in your life has prepared you to do this job well?

I was the oldest of nine and babysat a lot growing up. And I've always loved learning for learning's sake. As a youngster I enjoyed talking to adults and questioning them to death. So I don't have a problem with a kid who's asking 20 questions.

How do you think working in a special school differs from being an assistant at a mainstream school?

I think we form closer relationships with the kids. The children in my room stay there for three years. You get the chance to see and help a kid grow. And most of the children stay at this school for years.

What was the hardest aspect of working in this field at first?

Being accepted by teachers. When I started, the role of assistant was undefined. In my first job I used to go out and get coffee and doughnuts in the morning. One day I didn't go, and the teacher I worked with said she'd like some coffee. I said I hadn't planned to go out that day and that that wasn't my job anyway. She said that it was. I said, "You tell the principal I'm not going to go." The role of the assistant has since become clearer.

The other hard part was not really knowing about the special needs of autistic children, and what I learned I had to learn on my own. The teachers were allowed to read psychological information on individual students, but we assistants weren't allowed to see those files. That was frustrating. For example, if a particular kid didn't like jewelry and I tried to interact with that child while wearing a chain around my neck, it could spell trouble that could have been avoided.

How has your job evolved over the years?

My job hasn't changed a lot, but the profession is beginning to. Paraprofessionals are starting to be viewed as part of the education profession—just as paralegals are considered part of the legal profession. I'm the activities coordinator for the local American Federation of Teachers. We are helping educators to educate. What we would like to see is all assistants getting certified by acquiring a year of college, 30 credits. After all, LPNs (licensed practical nurses) are licensed. We feel certification would also help with our salaries.

What do you like most about your job?
It's nice when you see your kids come in with every problem you can name, all sorts of emotional baggage, and you can help them get rid of that and grow and lead a better life.

Have you done anything you're especially proud of?
For some reason, I've always liked the kids other people don't—the black sheep of the classroom. There was a girl from last year who used to call me dirty names when she was behaving badly. She didn't have a father at home, so I became the male figure in her life. I think that if I were running for mayor, and the kids had to vote, I'd make it.

What do you like least about what you're doing?
Being looked upon as not really part of the teaching profession. Last year I was the union representative for our building and even represented the teachers. But half of the teachers had trouble accepting me in that role. It's getting better, but it's not all there.

What would you tell someone who was thinking about becoming a teacher aide?
If I were looking to hire someone as a teacher assistant, I would lean toward someone who's done some sort of work with kids, in a day care center or babysitting. If you think you would like a career in education, become a teacher assistant first. It will help you make a more valid decision about what they want to do. It's also satisfying and rewarding work.

Michelle A. Hernandez, 21,
preschool teacher, The Lion's Den,
Atherton, California
Years in the field: three

How did you become a preschool teacher?
I took part in a program called Careers with Children that
was offered through the Regional Occupation Center at my
high school. During my junior year I had classes five days
a week for three hours on such things as how to work with
children and what to expect in terms of their behavior and
age.

The following year I went to different schools to get hands-
on experience. I assisted the teacher, and each week I
planned a particular project such as preparing a snack or
doing an art activity. I discussed my ideas with the teacher,
got the okay from her and then cleared it with my instructor. The fifth day of the week I went back to the classroom
to ask questions. At the end I received a certificate good
for nine early childhood education units.

**Was that all you needed to qualify as a preschool
teacher?**
No. I needed 12 units, so I took classes at two different
local colleges to get the rest of my training.

How did you decide you wanted to work with kids?
I wanted the little brothers and sisters I had never had.
When I would go to the house of a friend who had younger
brothers and sisters, I would always get down on the floor
and play with them. I like the idea of teaching kids to do
different things and seeing how happy they get when they
accomplish something new.

What was your first job working with children?
As soon as I finished high school I worked as a teacher
aide at a preschool. The children were four and five years
old, and there were two aides and two teachers. I set up art
activities that were planned by the teachers and did other
things to help them out. The experience taught me a lot
about how to deal with the different problems children
have. And I observed a lot, like how to do circle time—

when you put a group of children in a circle and tell stories, sing songs and have other group activities.

Why did you leave?
I wanted a situation in which I could plan the activities and have some control in the classroom, so I left after two years. Soon after I read about the opening for the job I now have. I applied for it and got it.

How does being the teacher differ from being the aide?
You're not being told what to do all the time. You still have to go to the director of your school and ask her what you can do, but my boss is great and doesn't limit me. On my very first day my director told me I could hold circle time. I was nervous but had gotten good ideas from watching the teachers at my first job.

What is your daily work routine like?
I start at 8 A.M., when kindergartners and first graders who attend the school that's on these same grounds come in for early morning day care. I'm with them until their classes start just before 9 A.M. Then the preschoolers come in; there are 21 of them. They have free time when they can do an art project by themselves that I've set up for them or they can play with toys. At 10:15 we all clean up the classroom. That's followed by circle time.

We have a snack, then the kids go out to play. Afterward, they do a project with the director; during that time I pass out whatever materials are needed and get the children ready—for instance, help them into their smocks if they're going to be working with paints.

My lunch break is from noon until two. The preschoolers leave at 2 P.M., and then we get kindergartners and first graders in for afternoon day care. Up until I leave at five P.M. there are different groups of kids coming and going for afternoon care.

What do you enjoy most about what you're doing?
I like to be with the children because although the routine is the same, every day the kids are different. I like to be their friend as well as their teacher. I like the hours. I especially appreciate my director and all the experience she's letting me get.

Do you ever have to deal with the children's parents?
Yes. If a child doesn't listen or has problems with another kid, I'll discuss this with the parents if I'm there when they come to pick up their child or I'll write them a note. Usually I'll give the parents suggestions about how they can help correct the situation. Many times parents will call and thank me for bringing problems to their attention.

What has your proudest achievement been?
At the end of the last school year the parents were saying they were really going to miss the preschool during the summer. I suggested to my director that we should have a summer program—and she asked me to plan and run it!

Can you offer any suggestions to young people who might be considering becoming a preschool teacher?
Make sure you have patience. If you're really interested in working with children, visit a school and see what they do there. Some people think it's all fun and games or just babysitting. It's not: It's planning and directing and supervising and assisting the children. If after you've observed some classes you still want to be a teacher, read all you can and take courses in child care and children's behavior.

MUSEUM OR AMUSEMENT PARK STAFFER

Can you think of no better way to spend a day than at an amusement park? Are you someone who enjoys poking around a museum that's designed for the young and the young at heart? Then maybe working in a museum or a park is for you, provided you love working with the public and have the patience of a saint— imagine being costumed as an elephant and having your trunk tugged on all day!

Keeping kids big and small entertained has become big business nationwide. There are hundreds of theme and amusement parks in this country as well as museums that cater to kids. They are staffed by people who have a special affinity for children because they must interact directly with their young visitors—explaining a science display to a group of Girl Scouts, helping youngsters in and out of roller

79

coaster cars, dressing up as Alice in Wonderland or Charlie Brown. These fun folk bring amusement and theme parks and children's museums to life.

The responsibilities of an amusement park or museum staffer vary greatly depending on your job and where you work. Museum staffers, often called educators or explainers, generally meet and greet visitors, roam the museum answering questions, conduct tours and demonstrations, direct museumgoers to bathrooms and first aid facilities, help lost kids become found and generally make sure everyone has a good time. Depending on the size of the museum, they may also collect tickets, hand out brochures and maps and even help set up displays and hands-on exhibits.

Employees of amusement parks typically have less varied duties, particularly in larger parks. Their jobs may consist solely of operating a specific ride (and making sure the ride stays in good and safe working order); selling tickets, concessions or souvenirs; dressing up as a character; or performing in a stage show. Because parks located in cold climates are not open year-round, the jobs in those parks may be seasonal; employees must find other employment during the off season. If you're really interested in making an amusement park more of a career, however, you may be able to find a job in the administrative offices when the park is closed to the public.

Many employees of both museums and amusement parks begin as part-timers or volunteers during summer vacations in high school, or on weekends. This is a great way to get a sneak peak at what the job is like. It will help you decide if you can deal with long hours, working on weekends and being confronted daily with hordes of kids— all for pay that may seem like peanuts. It can also help you get a foot in the door come hiring time.

If having a good time on the job is as important to you as padding your bank account, then working in a children's museum or at an amusement park may be just the thing for you. Even if your first job is a part-time, with experience and dedication you may move into a full-time position, managing the entire floor staff of a museum or all the ride operators, characters or concession workers at an amusement park. Wherever your job takes you, there's one guarantee: You'll have a ball getting there.

What You Need to Know

Both museum workers and amusement park staffers get their training on the job; however, the following can help:

❑ Some knowledge of the type of exhibits featured in the museum; for instance, knowing about art history and styles, artists and so forth (for museum educators)

❑ How museums work in terms of acquiring art and other exhibits (for museum educators)

❑ Familiarity with the developmental stages of children (to respond to kids' questions in age-appropriate ways, be familiar with their attention span, etc.)

Necessary Skills

❑ The ability to speak in front of small groups of children (and a sprinkling of adults)

❑ A knack for overseeing more than one thing at a time (for instance, making sure a ride is operating properly, the kids on it are behaving and the children waiting to ride are staying in line)

❑ Organizational skills—keeping groups of kids together and attentive

❑ Public relations skills—dealing with people patiently, enthusiastically and calmly

Do You Have What It Takes?

❑ A love of kids and an appreciation for the things they find interesting and amusing

❑ Friendly personality

❑ Patience

❑ A sense of humor

❑ Enthusiasm for whatever you're sharing with kids—be it a nifty science exhibit or a stomach-flipping roller coaster

❑ A thick skin (which comes in handy when an irritated museum or park visitor takes out their frustration on you)

Physical Attributes

❏ Stamina and fitness (chances are you'll be on your feet much of the day; theme park characters may also have to walk around in heavy costumes)

❏ Good personal hygiene (since you will be dealing with the public much of the day as a representative of your museum or park)

❏ People who dress up in costumes may need to have a certain look or be a certain height or build to fit the character they're portraying

Education

High school diploma usually not required, but may be helpful, particularly in museums that focus on science, history and the like.

Licenses Required

None

Job Outlook

Competition for jobs: somewhat competitive

Children's museums represent expanding employment opportunities: there are currently about 300 such museums in the United States and that number is increasing by about 50 a year. However, because museums are inclined to hire volunteers (and rarely have trouble finding them); full-and part-time jobs are often tough to get.

Job opportunities in amusement and theme parks are also abundant. Every metropolitan area of the United States is served by a major one. Although few new big-name parks are opening up, existing parks are constantly expanding, thus creating new jobs. In addition, there are hundreds of smaller, regional parks throughout the country.

Entry-level job: museum educator or explainer, or amusement or theme park staffer (including ride operator; concession, souvenir or ticket salesperson; performer; character)

◆ **The Ground Floor**

Beginners and Experienced Staffers

◆ **On-the-Job Responsibilities**

❏ Sell tickets, hand out maps and brochures

In museums:
❏ Conduct tours of museums and direct individuals and groups to points of interest in the park as well as to bathrooms, lost and found and first aid areas

In amusement parks:
❏ Collect tickets; assist kids onto rides, make sure they are secured in their seats and help them off; interact with the kids during the ride; monitor the ride constantly for mechanical problems
❏ Play a behind-the-scenes role with puppet or other shows featuring performers

Theme park characters:
❏ Roam the park, meeting and greeting visitors, handing out balloons, buttons and the like, perhaps give little kids piggyback rides and otherwise entertain anyone and everyone you see; sometimes participate in shows

The hours of museum and park employees vary widely, depending on the size of the facility, the time of year and the policies of their place of employment. Parks and museums are open at least one weekend day (and many are open on both Saturday and Sunday), so workers are often expected to work one or two weekend days. Many museums are closed on Mondays. Some smaller museums may be

◆ **When You'll Work**

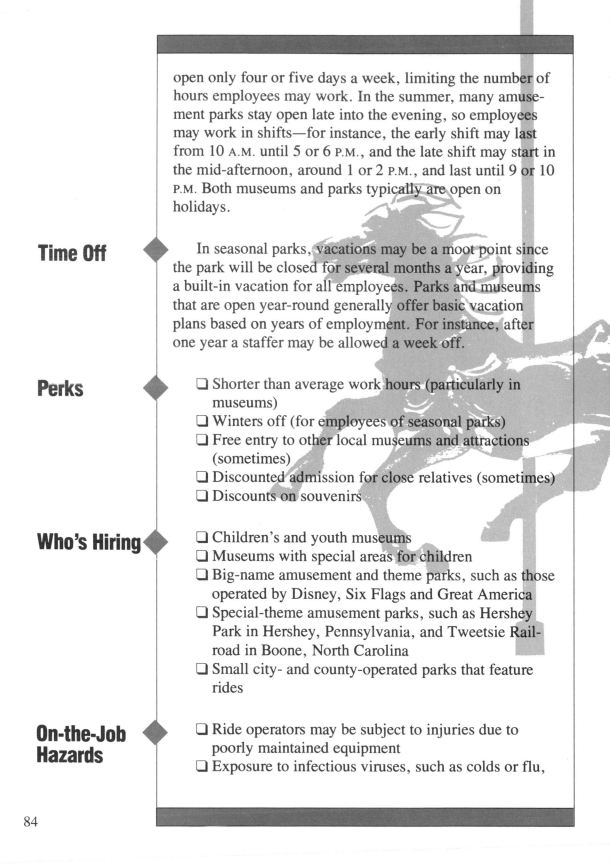

open only four or five days a week, limiting the number of hours employees may work. In the summer, many amusement parks stay open late into the evening, so employees may work in shifts—for instance, the early shift may last from 10 A.M. until 5 or 6 P.M., and the late shift may start in the mid-afternoon, around 1 or 2 P.M., and last until 9 or 10 P.M. Both museums and parks typically are open on holidays.

Time Off

In seasonal parks, vacations may be a moot point since the park will be closed for several months a year, providing a built-in vacation for all employees. Parks and museums that are open year-round generally offer basic vacation plans based on years of employment. For instance, after one year a staffer may be allowed a week off.

Perks

❑ Shorter than average work hours (particularly in museums)
❑ Winters off (for employees of seasonal parks)
❑ Free entry to other local museums and attractions (sometimes)
❑ Discounted admission for close relatives (sometimes)
❑ Discounts on souvenirs

Who's Hiring

❑ Children's and youth museums
❑ Museums with special areas for children
❑ Big-name amusement and theme parks, such as those operated by Disney, Six Flags and Great America
❑ Special-theme amusement parks, such as Hershey Park in Hershey, Pennsylvania, and Tweetsie Railroad in Boone, North Carolina
❑ Small city- and county-operated parks that feature rides

On-the-Job Hazards

❑ Ride operators may be subject to injuries due to poorly maintained equipment
❑ Exposure to infectious viruses, such as colds or flu,

through constant contact with the public
❑ Theme park characters who wear particularly heavy costumes and whose heads are completely covered by masks may be at risk for overheating and dehydration on very warm days

Surroundings

Museum staffers may work in large, many-roomed buildings amidst a wide variety of exhibits, from small, intimate hands-on displays to some that are bigger than life. On a busy day, museum employees may be constantly surrounded by people (and strollers and the like); on quiet days, things can be quite slow and boring.

People who work in amusement parks will also find that the crowds thin out as the weather cools down; ride operators, for instance, may sit for long periods with nothing to do. On busy days, however, parks hustle and bustle with kids and their families. The actual surroundings in a park vary; typically entire parks or specific areas are "decorated" according to a theme—such as a pirate ship, the old West or a fairy land. Everything from the waste baskets to the concession stands to the park benches may be designed to fit this theme.

Dollars and Cents

Most staffers in parks and museums are paid by the hour, and many make little more than their state's minimum wage. The truly dedicated may be able to pump up their earnings by working overtime. Employees who move on to become managers or supervisors usually draw a yearly salary, which varies according to the region, the size of the park or museum and their responsibilities.

Moving Up

Advancement opportunities in most parks and museums are few and far between. However, the employee who truly wants to develop a career in the field may sometimes do so through hard work, initiative and dedication, moving on to manage all part-timers and volunteers in a museum, for instance, or supervising all ride operators or costumed characters at a theme park. To secure a salaried job in the management area of museums and theme parks will usually require a return to college for a degree in management or a related area.

Where the Jobs Are

There are major amusement and theme parks throughout the United States, as well as many local parks. The majority of children's museums are located in the Northeast and in California, although they can also be found in many major United States cities.

Training

The majority of museum and park employees receive on-the-job training, which can range from a formal, structured orientation of the museum or park facilities to learn-as-you-go informal instruction.

The Male/Female Equation

Women dominate the field of museum workers, perhaps because traditionally they have gravitated toward careers in which the education of and interaction with kids is important. Both young men and women can be found in almost equal numbers in amusement and theme parks.

Making Your Decision: What to Consider

The Bad News

❑ Low pay, often no more than minimum wage
❑ Work schedule may include weekends
❑ During slow times things can get boring
❑ There is little opportunity for advancement

The Good News

❑ Admissions discounts
❑ Some museums close early in the day; park hours may be divided into shifts, meaning you could have mornings or afternoons off
❑ The work is usually downright fun
❑ Even entry-level employees may have some input into designing and constructing museum exhibits

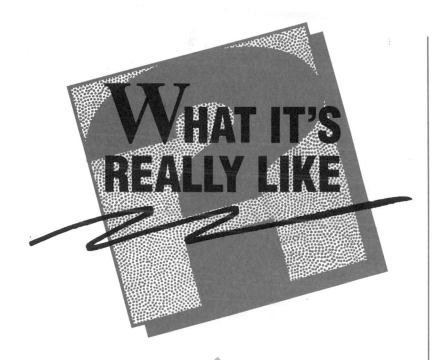

Gerri Wilson, 22,
recreation leader, Happy Hollow Park,
San Jose, California
Years in the field: five and a half

How did you get started?
I applied for work with the city of San Jose and was put on a waiting list. After several months I was offered a position as a recreation aide here at Happy Hollow Park.

As a recreation aide, what did you do?
I was a ride operator; my job was to operate the five different rides in this park, which are for small children. We have a small staff and on weekdays when there aren't many park visitors, an operator may be responsible for operating several rides; the parents and kids follow us around from ride to ride. I helped kids on and off the rides and entertained them while they rode by waving, encouraging them to ring the little bells and horns that are on the rides and so forth. I also had to make sure the rides were in good operating order.

Was it physically demanding?
During the summer we get quite a few visitors, and there

were times when I was constantly on my feet. It's not a sit-down type of job.

Did you have to wear a uniform?
Sort of—pants or shorts and a park-issue shirt and visor.

How important is it to like kids to be a ride operator?
You definitely have to like kids to do a job like this. You're in a public facility and the majority of the visitors are children. You have to care about them and what they're doing—you have to watch out for their safety.

Had you had much contact with children before taking this job?
I have a younger sister and nieces and nephews, so I've always been around smaller children. I babysat quite a bit as well, and I always thought I would work with kids.

Do most amusement park employees begin as ride operators?
This was a usual first job around here. You start off as a ride operator, then move into concessions. There are about 25 different positions you can work in.

What sort of training did you get?
The only training I got was from other employees who showed me how to operate the rides and explained the safety rules. Usually new employees, myself included, train on a ride called the Mini Putt, which consists of old fire engines and police cars that go around in a circle. The Mini Putt is the park's main attraction and it's the most difficult to handle in terms of crowd control. Then I went on to work the other rides for three or four days each.

What was hard about this type of work at first?
It was the first time I had worked in an amusement park, and I started during the summer when it's pretty busy. Each ride has an entrance gate and an exit gate, and you have to keep an eye on both of them at all times. We often got children who were eager to get on the ride. Kids would hop the gate while the ride was operating, and that's really dangerous. You have to take control, explain to the children that they're next in line without scaring them. It helped when the parents were there to reinforce that.

Did you ever have to discipline the kids?
If a child waiting in line became testy, we would explain to the parent what the rules were and have them do the disciplining.

Where did you go after being a ride operator?
My next step was rides manager: I made sure the ride operators were doing everything correctly, enforced the safety rules, gave the operators breaks and made sure the park in general was in tip-top operating condition. I had worked here eight or nine months when I became a manager. From there I started working in the concession stands doing cashiering. Then I went on to admissions; that involves handling large sums of money, escorting people into the park and so forth. Now I'm in administration.

Does that mean you have less contact with park visitors?
Yes, but I'm not completely cut off from the public. I answer phones a lot. I give out information on the park and directions for getting here, and I take reservations. But I also help handle first aid cases and lost children. For instance, if a kid gets lost and winds up at my office or if a parent comes in who can't find his or her child, I make an announcement over the PA system. When kids are brought in, they're often crying and panicked, and I try to calm them. From the beginning of February until the end of June we have group season, which brings a lot of school children here. I lead the groups into the park and help keep them separate from the other visitors.

What if someone is hurt?
We provide standard first aid and have minimal supplies; usually parents do the actual doctoring. If it's a serious injury, our responsibility is not to have physical contact, but to calm the child down and call for appropriate help. Because we're working with the public, we have to be certified in first aid and CPR.

Are you stuck in an office all the time?
No. I also do puppeteers on Wednesday and Thursday. At the park we use string puppets, marionettes and hand-rod puppets. We also perform traveling puppet shows at elementary schools.

What do you like most about what you're doing?
Being able to interact with the public, even though I do most of that on the phone now. I enjoy the public relations part of my job. We have a suggestion box, and we get quite a few compliments on the park, on the employees, how things are run, etc.

What don't you like?
During the off season when business slows down and the weather's getting cold there's not a lot to do. I'm the type of person who likes to keep busy constantly.

What advice would you give to someone planning to pursue a career at an amusement park?
Make sure you have lots of patience, understanding and a willingness to listen. Children will ask strange things and you have to know how to give them an answer they'll be able to understand. You definitely have to like children. Several employees who work here have had babysitting experience or are high school students who take child care classes. That sort of experience will help you in handling kids.

Lee Robinson, 34,
gallery manager, Please Touch Museum,
Philadelphia, Pennsylvania
Years in the field: One and a half

How did you get into the children's museum field?
I've been working with children since I was about 15. I worked at a daycare center at my church during the school year and at a camp in the summer. After high school I didn't consider working with kids because there wasn't much money involved, even though a lot of my friends would tell me that nothing put a sparkle in my eyes as much as talking about children did. A temporary agency sent me here to the museum to work in building maintenance; that was my official title, but I was always on the floor playing with the kids when I had time. They hired me full- time to do maintenance, but I was unhappy with that and resigned.

Two weeks later, before I actually left, this position opened up. The people who hired me had seen how I felt about the museum and how I was always involved with the children.

Is this a typical way to start—as a part-timer?
In this particular department of the museum we don't have any full-time positions besides mine. A lot of people start here part time and work their way up. We have several people who began as volunteers and now have paid jobs. That's a good way to get in and see how the museum operates.

What is your job like?
My role is to take care of the staffing of the floor. I make up the work schedules of the volunteers and paid staff, hire people (within my budget) and make sure the floor runs smoothly. We might have several floor activities going on at once, and I make sure they are manned properly. I spend about a third of my time on the floor. Officially my hours are 8:30 A.M. to 4:30 P.M., but I'm usually here till 6 or 7 P.M. finishing up paperwork.

How many people are you in charge of?
At present, approximately 13 paid staff and five or six volunteers.

Do you have any input into the types of exhibits featured at the museum?
Yes. Because I'm on the floor I see first hand how the kids respond to different exhibits, so I have some input in helping determine what types of things we'll put out.

What kind of preparation did you have for this type of work?
I've always had a desire to work with kids. My mom thought I was crazy when I began subscribing to parenting magazines and taking child development workshops in the ninth grade. I was always babysitting for my nephews.

Presently I'm also director of the Kids' Klub at my church. And I teach Sunday school.

Why do you enjoy interacting with children so much?
Children are much freer in their expression: They tell the truth right up front and I like that. You can do things with kids without feeling embarrassed or inhibited. I like know-

ing that someday they're going to think of me and smile. My goal is to have a positive influence on children.

What do you like least about what you're doing?
I would say sitting at the desk is my least favorite part. That's why I try to do paperwork during off hours. When the museum is open, I like to spend time on the floor with the staff or children.

Is there anything you've done here that you're particularly proud of?
There's a little girl named Leah who comes here often. One day I told her she could be the director of the museum. She is so committed and serious about her "position" here. Her mother tells me I have a friend for life. When Leah comes here she's right by my side; I like having such a positive impact on her.

You haven't been at this job very long. Are you finding any aspect of it particularly difficult?
Getting used to being a manager and being responsible for other people. I'm still working out the bugs. I tend to be laid-back and easygoing. Fortunately, I haven't had to fire anyone. Prior to my taking this job there was a lot of turnover, and management was interested in hiring me so that I could help stabilize the staff. I have, and I'm definitely proud of that.

What advice would you give to a young person interested in working in a children's museum?
Working with children is not for everyone—kids are very demanding and take a lot of energy. They can wear you out. I would strongly suggest volunteering at a recreation center, trying a couple of different ages to see if you really like it. You'll probably find one age will click better for you than all the others. If you decide you like working with kids, then go right in and apply at a museum. Different museums call entry-level positions different things: education assistants, tour guides, explainers. Even if no jobs are open, you can always volunteer and get a foot in the door that way.

Mike Dempsey, 25,
knight and assistant trainer,
Medieval Times Dinner and Tournament,
Buena Park, California
Years in the field: four

What is Medieval Times?
We recreate an eleventh-century dinner and tournament,
with knights competing in a sword fight and demonstrating
jousting, hand-to-hand combat and lance and javelin
throwing—all on horseback. The audience eats a typical
medieval meal while all this is going on.

How did you land this job?
I was working at a store, and one of the regular customers
was a knight here at Medieval Times. We got to talking
about it, and he suggested I come down and try out for
a job.

What was involved in trying out?
Because everything is done on horseback, they have you
get on a horse and take it through the different gaits. You
don't have to know how to ride already; in fact I had never
been on a horse before and was sort of scared of them. But
you have to show you have potential. That's all there was
to trying out, besides meeting some other requirements.

What were those?
You have to be at least 18 years old, in good physical condition, coordinated and pretty athletic. They also try to hire
people who are about the same height and build.

What was the training like?
Just like in the Middle Ages. You start out as a squire.
You're pretty much in the service of the knights—you take
care of their weapons, horses, get everything ready for
battle. There's also a head trainer who has been here for 15
years; he trains the horses and teaches the squires how to
fight. The knights also teach newcomers how to ride and to
use the weapons. There are five or six different weapons,
and you start out learning to use a sword, then the mace
and the axe, and then the others fall into place. The training
goes on during the day. At night, by observing the show,

we learn what happens and in what order. On average it takes three to six months to learn everything; it probably took me four months.

How many shows do you do each week?
I work six nights a week. On the weekend, I might work two or three shows in one day. A show lasts approximately two hours.

What sort of preparation did you have for this job?
I played sports in high school, so I was in good shape. It's almost good that I didn't know how to ride a horse: They find it easier to teach beginners how to ride like the knights did, using your legs to control the horse rather than the reins since you're usually holding a weapon.

And I've always been interested in the Middle Ages and have read a lot of books about that period throughout my life. Of course, I've learned a lot more since I've been here—one of our employees is very knowledgeable.

Do you have much contact with kids?
Not so much during the show, but we often go out and entertain kids—visit hospitals and do demonstrations for children in cancer wards, for instance. We once took a horse and two knights to a school and did a presentation just to give them a taste of what we do here at Medieval Times.

What was the hardest thing about doing this job in the beginning?
Learning how to handle the weapons. Anyone can pick up a sword and swing it around, but it takes a lot of practice to do it correctly. Surprisingly, I didn't have much trouble learning to ride. After a month of being around the horses I was okay.

What do you do as an assistant trainer?
I got this position two or three months ago, when the former assistant left to become a teacher. They asked me to fill the position and I accepted.

When we get new trainees in, I start teaching them the basics—take them through how to hold the sword, handle it, the moves of the swordplay. The head trainer takes it from there and helps polish up their act.

What do you like most about what you're doing?
I like the audience participation and the crowd reaction to the show. It's almost like being a superstar. People ask for your autograph and to have their picture taken with you. It's like having a little celebrity status: It's fun to be recognized at places like the Laundromat.

What do you like least?
Nothing: If I didn't like it, I wouldn't be here. In fact, they open new castles every few years, and I've traveled around to help train the new people. I wouldn't mind relocating to a new castle.

Have you done anything you're especially proud of in your work?
I do a lot of interviews with the press. Sometimes I do media blitzes up and down the coast, talking to television reporters. And we were in the Rose Parade not long ago.

What advice would give to someone thinking of working in a theme park?
The first thing I'd say is to check it out to make sure it's something you'd really want to do. Then go out and try to get some experience. Do anything that you feel would help you prepare.

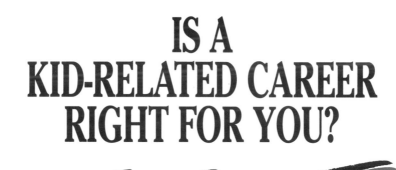

IS A KID-RELATED CAREER RIGHT FOR YOU?

Before you sign up for a program of study or start to look for one of the jobs described in this book, it's smart to figure out whether that career will be a good fit, given your background, skills and personality. There are several ways to do this assessment. They include:

❑ Talk to people who already work in the field. Find out what they like and don't like about their jobs, what kinds of people their employers hire and what their recommendations are about training. Ask if there are any books or publications that would be helpful for you to read. Maybe you could even "shadow" the workers for a day as they go about their duties.

❑ Use a computer to help you identify career options. Some of the most widely used software programs are *Discover,* by the American College Testing Service; *SIGI Plus,* developed by the Educational Testing Service; and *Career Options,* by Peterson's. Some public libraries make this career software available to library users at little or no cost. The career counseling or guidance offices of your high school or local community college are other possibilities.

❑ Take a vocational interest test. The most common are the Strong-Campbell Interest Inventory and the Kuder Occupational Interest Survey. High schools and colleges usually offer free testing to students and alumni at their guidance and career planning offices. Many career counselors in private practice or at community job centers can also give the test and interpret the results.

❑ Talk to a career counselor. You can find one by asking friends and colleagues if they know of any good ones. Or contact the career information office of the adult education division of a local college. Its staff and workshop leaders often do one-on-one counseling. The job information services division of major libraries sometimes offer low- or no-cost counseling by appointment. Or check the *Yellow Pages* under the heading "Vocational Guidance."

But first, before you spend your time, energy or money doing any of the above, take one or more of the following five quizzes (one for each career discussed in this book). The results can help you evaluate whether you have the basic traits and abilities that are important to success in that career—in short, if you are cut out for the job.

If becoming a caregiver interests you, take this quiz:

Read each statement, then choose the number 0, 5 or 10. The rating scale below explains what each number means.

> **0** = Disagree
> **5** = Agree somewhat
> **10** = Strongly agree

____I am familiar or am willing to learn how infants, toddlers and preschoolers develop physically, emotionally and intellectually

____I know or am willing to learn the fundamentals of child care—changing diapers, preparing bottles and meals and feeding babies and young children, supervising naps, etc.

97

___I have a knack for playing with youngsters

___I have the ability to relate well to children and parents

___I know how to monitor a child in terms of safety, am familiar with or willing to learn first aid basics and CPR (cardiopulmonary resuscitation)

___I am familiar with strollers, car seats and other equipment for children

___I know what to do to keep a child from hurting him- or herself

___I am able to help a child work through his or her frustrations while keeping my own in check

___I truly enjoy being around babies and little kids

___I am in good health and am fit enough to handle the physical rigors of child care—bending, lifting, chasing after toddlers

Now add up your score.   ___Total points

If you scored less than 50, then you probably do not have enough interest in children or knowledge of how they must be looked after to become a caregiver. If your points totaled between 50 and 75, you may have the necessary love and patience for youngsters to be able to care for them, but you may want to further develop your caregiving skills—perhaps through a nanny school or by taking some continuing education courses. If you scored over 75 points, consider yourself a prime candidate for securing a job as a nanny or day care center employee, or for starting your own family day care business.

If you are interested in becoming a children's recreation instructor, take this quiz.

Read each statement, then choose the number 0, 5 or 10. The rating scale below explains what each number means.

0 = Disagree
5 = Agree somewhat
10 = Strongly agree

___I am familiar with the differences among children in

terms of physical capabilities, coordination, attention span and ability to follow instructions

——I have a flair for motivating children and keeping them interested

——I can discipline youngsters effectively

——I am capable of teaching children through verbal explanation and physical demonstration

——I can control and watch over a number of children at once

——I know the basics of safety and first aid, or am willing to learn; I have or am interested in obtaining training in CPR (cardiopulmonary resuscitation)

——I have ample knowledge of and skill in a particular sport or activity

——I am energetic and enthusiastic

——I enjoy kids and do not lose patience with them

——I am in good physical condition

Now add up your score. ——Total points

If you scored less than 50, then you probably do not have enough interest or skill to teach children a sport or other activity. If you scored between 50 and 75 points, with further investigation and perhaps experience interacting with children, you may do very well as a recreation instructor. If your score was 75 points or more, you have the necessary skills, flair for teaching and love of kids to be a first-rate recreation instructor.

If working in a toy store or hobby shop appeals to you, take this quiz:

Read each statement, then choose the number 0, 5 or 10. The rating scale below explains what each number means.

0 = Disagree
5 = Agree somewhat
10 = Strongly agree

——I have some knowledge of the developmental stages of

children in terms of their cognitive (thinking) and verbal skills and manual dexterity

____I have a basic understanding of what types of toys are appropriate for children of different ages

____I am personable and find it easy to get along with many types of people

____I would not get rattled or impatient with a hard-to-please, complaining or indecisive customer

____I really enjoy playing with toys or certain hobby materials

____I am able to handle money and basic business transactions, such as running a cash register or processing a credit card

____I am punctual and trustworthy

____I am comfortable taking orders

____I don't mind pitching in to help with even menial tasks

____I would be able to remember names and faces of regular customers, what ages their kids are and what sorts of toys they tend to seek out

Now add up your score.   ____Total points

If your total points were less than 50, you probably do not have enough interest in toys, kids or the world of retail to work in a toy store or hobby shop. If your total points were between 50 and 75, you may have an interest in toys, but may lack some sales pizzazz, knowledge of how kids grow and develop, and what toys are safe and appealing to children of different ages—all of which can be acquired. If you scored more than 75 points, you're right on track to secure a job as a toy or hobby store salesperson.

If you are interested in a career as a preschool teacher or teacher aide, take this quiz:

Read each statement, then choose the number 0, 5 or 10. The rating scale below explains what each number means.

0 = Disagree

5 = Agree somewhat

10 = Strongly agree

____I am familiar with how schools are organized and operate and enjoy the classroom atmosphere

____I know the fundamentals of reading, writing, science, grammar and other basic school subjects

____I have some knowledge of how children of different ages develop intellectually, socially, physically and emotionally

____I have a repertoire of games and other activities for children of different ages

____I have a knack for conveying information in ways children can understand and absorb

____I know how to conduct group activities

____I am comfortable with groups of children and am able to command their attention and monitor their behavior

____I am skilled at filing, record keeping and using office and audiovisual equipment, or am willing to learn

____I enjoy children and possess great patience when dealing with them

____I am healthy and physically fit and would have no trouble keeping up with active youngsters

Now add up your score.   ____Total points

If you came up with fewer than 50 points, a career in the classroom is probably not for you. If your total points added up to between 50 and 75, you may have what it takes to work with students, but you would be wise to investigate the field further—perhaps by visiting classrooms with children of different ages to get a feel for the job. If you scored more than 75 points, you definitely have what it takes to become an A + preschool teacher or teacher aide.

If you think you would like to work in a children's museum or at an amusement park, take this quiz.:

Read each statement, then choose the number 0, 5 or 10. The rating scale below explains what each number means.

0 = Disagree
5 = Agree somewhat
10 = Strongly agree

___I am able to interact with kids of different ages in ways that will entertain as well as educate them

___I am comfortable speaking in front of groups of people

___I am good at "herding" groups of kids and keeping them together and involved

___I would welcome the opportunity to know more about art, science, history and other subjects that are often featured in children's museums

___I don't mind being on the job on Saturday and/or Sunday, for instance

___I am fit and would be able to walk, bend, lift up kids and perform other physical tasks comfortably

___I am by nature cheerful and enthusiastic, and I enjoy meeting new people

___I have an eyes-in-the-back-of-my-head knack for watching over several things at once

___I do not take it personally when others vent their frustrations on me; likewise, I don't let my problems affect my demeanor and attitude while on the job

___I enjoy working outside and would not mind wearing a costume or honoring rules regarding how I dress and groom myself

Now add up your score.   ___Total points

If your score added up to less than 50 points, chances are you are not cut out for working in an amusement park or kids' museum. If your total points were between 50 and 75, you probably have what it takes to pursue a museum or amusement park career, but you may want to familiarize yourself more with how youngsters of various ages like to be dealt with and practice your people skills. If you scored above 75 points, you most likely have what it takes to become a museum educator or amusement park staffer and should be able to handle the training involved in either career with aplomb.

ABOUT THE
AUTHOR

Maura Rhodes Curless is a freelance writer and editor whose work has appeared in such publications as *Self, Redbook, McCall's* and *American Health.* She is the author of *Fitness,* also in the Careers Without College series. She was formerly a senior editor at *Health* magazine, where she was responsible for features on parenting, children's health and well-being, as well as fitness, nutrition and psychology. She lives in Scarsdale, New York, and is the mother of a two-year-old son.